ADA-4758

GP

D0401248

with Matthew Margolis

The Good Life: Your Dog's First Year

Grrr: The Complete Guide to Understanding and Preventing Aggressive Behavior in Dogs

Solutions for Your Dog and You

The Ultimate Guide to Dog Training

The Golden Years: A Pet Owner's Guide to the Golden Retriever

The Good Shepherd: A Pet Owner's Guide to the German Shepherd Dog

Woof! The Funny and Fabulous Trials and Tribulations of 25 Years as a Dog Trainer

I Just Got a Puppy. What Do I Do?

When Good Dogs Do Bad Things

Underdog

Good Dog, Bad Dog

How To Buy, Train,

Understand, and Enjoy

Your New Kitten

A Fireside Book
Published by Simon & Schuster
New York   London   Toronto   Sydne

I JUST GOT A KITTEN.

What Do I Do?

Mordecai Siegal

Photographs by Ginger S. Buck

FIRESIDE
Rockefeller Center
1230 Avenue of the Americas
New York, NY 10020

For information about special discounts for bulk purchases,
please contact Simon & Schuster Special Sales at
1-800-456-6798 or business@simonandschuster.com.

Designed by Jaime Putorti

Manufactured in the United States of America

10   9   8   7   6   5   4   3   2   1

ISBN-13: 978-0-7432-4509-8
ISBN-10:   0-7432-4509-1

To all the cats I've loved before,
who traveled in and out my door.
I'm glad they took a look,
And stayed to write this book.

To Max and Texas and to Alice
who always drooled on me with love

Acknowledgments

My deepest gratitude goes to Tara Parsons, who is not only a wonderful editor but also a kind and generous soul. She has been my advocate as well as the champion of this book through some tough times, and did not waver. I wish all deserving writers could be blessed with such an editor. She is a rare one.

I will never forget the special consideration and expressions of respect from David Rosenthal, executive vice president and publisher of Simon & Schuster, that came precisely when I needed it most. We go back a ways in the whirl of good books and I can safely say this one exists only because of his goodwill.

Ah, and then there's Mel Berger of the William Morris Agency, who gets personally involved even when he tries to avoid it. What would I ever do without him? Thanks for everything, Mel.

To Allene Tartaglia, director of special events, the Cat Fanciers' Association, for all her advice and concern given so generously at the beginning of this project, which seems like such a long time ago.

Many thanks also to Kent Highhouse, cat lover supreme, for his help during the creation of this book.

Thomas H. Dent, executive director of the Cat Fanciers'

Association has been over the many years a true friend and an important source of help and information regarding this obsession of ours with cats. I don't know who I owe more, Tom or Allene.

And many thanks to G. Allen Scruggs, author and consummate Japanese Bobtail breeder, who has been a true friend over the years.

I must also express my sincere gratitude to the Ladies of the Perfect Purr for their friendship and advice. They are: Pam DelaBar, president of the Cat Fanciers' Association and CFA show judge; Kitty Angell, CFA vice president and show judge; Joan Miller, CFA legislative coordinator and show judge; Pat Jacobberger, CFA show judge; Carol Krzanowski, managing editor, *CFA Almanac*; and Dr. Susan Little, CFA and Winn Feline Foundation activist.

CONTENTS

The Kitten Is Here. What Do I Do? Help!

Do not panic. Remember, new kittens are a joy, especially if you are a mature, capable cat owner and you treat your new kitten with love and respect. *I Just Got a Kitten* can help you with all the questions that will arise now and in the next year. Here is an immediate, handy list of what you will need for your new feline. For further details and advice, read through the chapters, preferably starting with Chapter One.

- If possible, prepare in advance the various essentials and comforts for your new kitten: food, water, litter, a litter pan, and a cat bed or blanket. See Chapter Four for details.
- Make friends. Handle your kitten affectionately. Create a loving relationship. See Chapter Five.

- Feed your kitten. He's probably hungry. See Chapter Eight.
- Show him where his litter pan is and teach him how to use it. See Chapter Nine.
- If he scratches, if he does things you want him to stop doing—such as climbing up the curtains—learn how to address these issues from the very start. See Chapter Ten.
- Calm down. Put the kitten to bed and go to sleep. Tomorrow will be an exciting day with more to do. This is fun!

Introduction

Leonardo da Vinci said, "The smallest feline is a master-piece." Leonardo was right. Kittens *are* beautiful and fascinating creatures, and a loving addition to any family. A kitten's love can be as comforting as buttered potatoes and rice pudding and as soothing as meditation and a Spanish guitar. In times of stress, the petite feline can actually lower your blood pressure and make you laugh. It is amazing how such a small creature has the ability to create feelings of contentment as well as to fashion a warm and happy environment in your home. It's essential to give your kitten the right start, with a sure hand, in order to create this pretty picture of contentment.

The musical *Cats* may have closed on Broadway, but kittens are still performing in home theaters. They are child stars, stand-up comedians, and sit-down dinner guests. But in his quest for pleasure and adventure, a frisky kitten can also create stress if you don't understand him and learn how to handle his playful but mischievous ways. When a kitten leaps off your shelf, he may knock over your bottle of vitamins as he flies through the air to the kitchen table below, with paws landing in your cereal bowl creating a tidal wave of milk, flakes, and bananas. No pressure there, right? Kittens can and often do make crashing noises in the middle of the night, scratch up the furniture, knock things down, and chew valuable objects (or dangerous ones). Depending on the breed, they can also be a walking talk show, playing the parts of controlling host, chatty guest, and dutiful sidekick all rolled into one.

Your new kitten will jump, run, bump; he will pierce whatever appeals to him with his needlelike teeth; he will sleep most of the day and play through the night. He has a special set of needs and desires when it comes to eating and relieving himself. A kitten can get into everything as he explores his new home, from precious knickknacks to freshly laundered clothes, and just as you think you've had it, the baby cat will curl up on your chest and fall asleep, a portrait of innocence.

The cat owner in search of the perfect purr has many books to choose from. However, there is little available for the inexperienced person with a new kitten. Kitten information is usually offered as a small slice of a cat book. It is essential though for new cat owners to fully understand their kittens' nature and needs and respond accordingly, lest the days of catnip and roses be spoiled by a full-grown, misbehaving cat. It's not easy: kittens are irresistible and every one of them has the ability to make us prisoners of our own emotions. That does not mean you cannot take charge of the situation and make life better for yourself and the new addition to your home. You might turn to a veterinarian or an animal behaviorist, or you can simply thumb through *I Just Got a Kitten. What Do I Do?* to learn how to create happy days and nights for the new babe in your life.

THE BIRTH OF A KITTEN

The birth of a kitten is one of the most moving events you can see. New life offers an opportunity to enjoy innocence, trust, and love generously given. It is also a marker to the temperament of your new pet.

As a kitten grows into an adult, some aspects of its disposition actually depend on its very first moments of birth. It is easy to understand how inherited behavior and breed characteristics combined to create that kitten in your arms. What is seldom considered is how an easy or difficult birth and first hours of life can impact your kitten's capacity for survival, which includes seeking warmth, food, and safety. It helps a great deal to understand the implications of those first few hours of life and longer. Understanding will help you cope with "cat problems" with patience, kindness, and effectiveness. A kitten that was born easily and with no complications, that was never bullied by its littermates when seeking its mother's warmth and milk is certain to have a sweeter, more delightful personality. If the opposite is the case, the kitten may grow into a shy, timid, fearful, or even aggressive cat.

To help you understand this development, here is a brief description of how your kitten entered the world. To begin with, breeders and experienced cat people refer to delivering kittens as *queening*. Veterinary textbooks refer to it as *parturition*. When the mother cat, called the *queen*, is about to deliver her kittens, which happens sometime between day 64 and 69 of pregnancy, she finds a quiet, dimly lit, secluded place to nest and prepares herself for the event. A thoughtful cat owner or breeder provides her with pillows and blankets and stays available to help as needed.

As she goes into labor, she will experience contractions of the uterus. She may assume a squatting position as she would in her cat box or she may lie on her side. In a normal delivery, the first kittens are born quickly after a bit of straining to expel them, one by one. During this phase of delivery, one or two kittens may leave her body. They may be facing forward or backward (breech position) as they travel through the birth canal. Occasionally a kitten will travel down the birth canal in a breech position and cause a blockage, which may require professional help. Other causes of blockages may be that the mother has a narrow or fractured pelvis, that the kitten's head is not in the proper position, that an individual kitten's *placenta* did not get expelled from the mother's body, or that the kitten is unusually large. If a blockage occurs with the first kitten, it can become a serious matter for those yet to be born.

The newborns will be encased in an *amniotic sac*, which is a thin membrane wrapped around each kitten individually like a form-fitted plastic bag. Attached to the sac is an *umbilical cord*, which goes directly into the *placenta*, a small mass that provides nourishment and oxygen to each fetus as it develops within the mother throughout pregnancy. The *umbilical cord* is a pipeline between the placenta and the fetus. Each fetus has its own placenta and umbilical cord. The placenta leaves the queen's body following the birth of each kitten, but several minutes may pass before this happens.

Mama cat is supposed to lick each newborn vigorously, which stimulates independent breathing. She tears the membrane of the amniotic sac with her teeth and peels it away once the newborn kitten is out of her body. During this process she removes the sac and consumes the placenta and a good bit of the cord once it is out. This allows the kitten to start breathing. The next kitten or kittens may not arrive for another hour, for six hours, or, as in some extreme cases, for twenty-four hours. In the meantime, the first to arrive, without sight or hearing, will crawl to find its mother's body for the warmth, find a nipple, and start nursing before the other kittens are born. This is how a normal delivery occurs.

A troubled delivery may consist of:

- Labor that continues for more than six hours before the kittens are born.
- An interval of several hours between the delivery of each kitten.
- A kitten that is lodged in the birth canal and partially visible.
- A blockage in the birth canal.
- Failure by the queen to peel away the membrane that encases the kitten.
- Failure by the queen to stimulate the kitten with her tongue in order to promote independent breathing.

An experienced cat breeder will call a veterinarian if labor is unproductive for more than six hours. When a newborn is somewhat visible but is lodged in the birth canal, the breeder will grasp the kitten as gently as possible and firmly pull it down from the base of the queen's tail and out of her body. When the breeder cannot do this, a veterinarian must do it as soon as possible. If the queen for some reason fails to remove the membrane encasing the newborn, the breeder must quickly tear it open starting at the face and peel it off the entire body. This will enable the kitten to breathe independently and avoid suffocation. The breeder will then have to wipe away the fluid from the kitten's mouth and nostrils with a moistened cloth to facilitate breathing. This is not difficult but does require a delicate touch.

As stressful as these situations may be for the mother cat, they may be even more stressful for the kittens. These are physically harrowing events and they can have an indelible influence on a kitten's personality. If a kitten's first moments

of life involve a struggle to breathe or some other physical trauma, the stage could be set for a less-than-desirable adult temperament. A kitten that is among the last to be born and is prevented from getting to the mother by the others in the litter, even for a short time, or cannot find its way may become a shy, timid, or aggressive cat. Understanding this trauma will help you to adjust your own behavior when relating to your pet and then to implement appropriate techniques for altering your pet's unwanted behavior.

If you are not able to be present at its birth, you can still identify your cat's temperament (see Chapter Two, on selecting a kitten) and respond accordingly by being an understanding and nurturing friend and caregiver as your kitten grows into a mature cat.

HERE, KITTY, KITTY: SELECTING A KITTEN

Which one? Which one? They are all so adorable. Making a choice can be a nail-biter. This is the first important decision a cat owner must make and it's a doozy. So there you are looking down at a litter of kittens. (If you're lucky, the mother or father cat is around somewhere and you can get a good look at what the kittens might be like as adults.) But wait a moment. Looks can be a compelling feature, but in terms of cat ownership, they are far less significant than a kitten's health and its temperament. Besides, there is no such thing as an unattractive kitten!

So let's get to the preliminaries leading up to your actual choice. Here are a few questions that you should ask yourself before looking at kittens. First, do you want a pedigreed kitten of a specific breed registered with a cat registering organization such as the Cat Fanciers' Association (CFA) or one of undetermined lineage, a nonpedigreed kitten? Do you want a male or a female kitten? Long-haired or short-haired? An active cat or a layabout? An aloof cat or one that likes to cozy up? The wise person looks beyond kittenhood and tries to see the cat the kitten will become.

Pedigreed Kittens

Predictability is the key factor here. When you choose a Siamese or a Persian, for example, you pretty much know what you are getting and how the kitten will turn out as an adult. You only have to look at a photo of a typical example of a breed to know what it should look like as an adult cat. You can see its body shape, size, length of coat, coat patterns allowed, varieties of coat colors, head shape, and various other factors that will have some bearing on your choice. If you talk to an experienced breeder or someone who knows the breed, you can certainly learn a great deal about a cat's temperament: how it will behave as an adult. Some breeds are very active, while others are more or less sedentary. Some like to walk around with you wherever you go, while others may be distant, choosing when they wish to relate to you. Some breeds are quite "talkative," while others hardly utter a sound, and when they do, it is a barely audible mew.

Some breeds, Persians for example, are somewhat docile and quite easygoing, as a breed. However, whether a specific Persian adjusts to humans or not, learns to catch mice, and so on, depends on what it has inherited from its parents; from environmental influences, such as being taught by the mother cat; and from early socialization with human beings. In these matters, a nonpedigreed kitten has the same possibilities as a pedigreed kitten, including some of the behavioral characteristics from one of the breeds in the blend.

According to the Cat Fanciers' Association, the world's largest registry of pedigreed cats, the term *pedigreed cat* "usually refers to a cat whose heritage is known, documented and registered." CFA defines a pedigree as "a form on which a cat and its background is recorded for three generations back." Pedigreed cats that meet all show rules may compete in sanctioned cat shows and are eligible for breeding programs and registration in a cat registering organization such as the CFA.

A pedigreed cat can be surprisingly expensive to purchase from a breeder, depending on whether it is to be a show cat, a breeding cat, or a house pet.

Nonpedigreed Kittens or Kittens of No Specific Breed

These constitute the majority of all cats here and throughout the world. They are the most beloved of all cats. In North America, pet owners refer to them as house cats, alley cats, everyday cats, all-purpose cats, Heinz 57 Varieties, domestic shorthairs, or domestic longhairs. In England, pet owners lovingly refer to them as *moggs*. No matter what you call them, they are unregistered, nonpedigreed, and not representative of any particular cat breed. In most cases, their ancestry is unknown beyond the previous generation, if that. They are the result of random matings of various cat breeds or of cats of the same background.

Despite the many and varied good looks of nonpedigreed cats, no established cat registering organization will accept one for competition in sanctioned cat shows, except in the household pet division. To qualify for entry in a CFA show, household pets must be neutered (except for kittens), must have all their physical properties (except for a tail in the case of an unregistered Manx), and may not be declawed. Show judges evaluate them based on physical condition, cleanliness, presentation, temperament, and attractive or unusual appearance. In cat shows, an official cat judge examines all pedigreed cats in competition and compares each to a written breed standard.

The issues of health and behavior in nonpedigreed cats (as with all cats) have everything to do with their individual genetic predisposition for specific forms of behavior in addition to the impact of their experiences with other animals, including cats, dogs, littermates, and most importantly, with humans. It is rare that anyone knows about a nonpedigreed kitten's ancestors unless the kitten's parents are available for observation. You will want to closely monitor its interactions with nearby littermates.

Keep in mind that nonpedigreed kittens are in such abundance that the cost for one can be anywhere from zero to a one-hundred-dollar donation to an animal shelter.

The Male Cat

Typically, the male is larger than the female and may be more nervous in some situations. The male's sexual status influences its behavior to a great degree. A *whole* male cat, one that has not been sexually altered by surgery, is more likely than a female to wander from home whenever the opportunity arises. This is especially the case if there is an unspayed female close by that is in *heat*. He will soon be part of a *clowder* of males waiting for the opportunity to mate with the ladies in the neighborhood. Sooner or later, he will fight with the other males. Whole male cats are definitely more aggressive and clash with other males over sexual rights, territory, and social rank.

Unaltered males are usually more independent and somewhat aloof. They can become unsettled and upset if they do not mate on a regular basis. Such males can hear or smell a female in heat from a great distance and will pace back and forth vigorously, make a constant, loud, throaty growl, and make every effort to get to her for the purpose of mating.

Sexual maturity develops early in cats—by six to eight months of age for some—and can present disturbing problems for the uninitiated cat owner. Male cats that have not been altered will at an early age begin backing up against a wall or vertical object and spraying sexually scented urine. This behavior is referred to as *spraying*. It is an instinctual behavior designed to attract females as well as claim territory. It creates an unpleasant odor that is difficult to eradicate. The wise pet owner has the male cat sexually altered (castrated) by a veterinarian at approximately six months of age to avoid this behavior before it starts.

The Female Cat

Living in the wild, most of the larger cat species of both sexes travel alone. The sexes behave similarly except during mating, pregnancy, and the rearing of cubs. Both males and females keep pretty much to themselves, maintaining separate territories and hunting ranges where possible. They hunt and feed alone and form no permanent relationships. Lions, the exception to this rule, live in a loose arrangement called a *pride*. The general rule pretty much applies to domestic cats as well. They will live together with other cats and will form a loosely defined social pecking order if that is the situation in which they must live. There is such a thing as a top cat; it can be a male or a female, depending on size, age, and experience. Of course, a female with a litter of kittens can be formidable, even to the largest male cat.

Females are less likely to wander off unless they are in heat. They are usually more affectionate and purr at the slightest touch. Females seem to want more attention from humans than males, and they are usually more companionable.

An unspayed female characteristically goes into *estrus* (heat) approximately twice a year, although some cats experience this state of sexual receptivity on a continual basis, perpetually ready to mate and to conceive. Female behavior changes radically and surprisingly to the inexperienced cat owner during the estrous cycle. Humans exposed to this behavior for the first time may become frightened or disturbed. Sometimes sexual behaviors are confused with illness. A female will vocalize in a variety of ways from demure purring to loud, throaty meows, all designed to attract the attention of the local males. Sometimes she sounds as if she were in pain. Even her posture may change. A female in heat will frequently lie stretched out, rubbing herself against the floor or carpet as she would if male cats were present. During estrus, the female cat secretes an odorous fluid intended to attract sexually capable males for the purpose of mating.

None of these behaviors remain once the female is surgically altered, which should take place at approximately six months of age.

A Healthy Kitten

There is nothing more heartbreaking than learning to love a cat only to lose it early on to poor health. Veterinary care for a sickly cat can be expensive. You owe it to yourself to choose a kitten with the best chance of a long, healthy life. If you carefully observe the physical appearance and behavior of kittens, you can improve your chances for making a wise choice.

Few serious cat breeders will give up a kitten before it is three months of age. However, this timetable is often impractical, especially for nonpedigreed kittens, which can be difficult to place in good, loving homes. Unfortunately, there are more kittens than there are homes for them.

Kittens begin to be weaned away from their mother's milk at approximately four weeks of age and by eight weeks are eating whole food entirely, or at least a combination of the two. It really depends on who is in charge—a nursing mama cat, a cat breeder, or an inexperienced backyard breeder. Mama cats usually do not allow kittens to nurse indefinitely. Four to six weeks is about all they permit, if that long. Breeders and experienced cat owners begin feeding baby food or tiny bits of meat by the third or fourth week and gradually increase this diet as interest in mama's milk wanes.

A fully weaned kitten usually sustains the transition from the litter to the new home best. Examine your prospective kitten's mouth and look for a full set of bright, pointed teeth set in clear pink gums. If the teeth have only partially emerged, the kitten has not yet completed teething and it should remain with Mom. The teeth are normal if they mesh properly, with the upper incisors meeting the bottom incisors evenly. Incisors are the twelve small teeth in the front of the mouth, which should be present by the fourth week: six uppers and six lowers. All twenty-six baby teeth should be present by the sixth week of age.

A kitten's coat should be clean, have a slight shine, and certainly be free of ticks, fleas, lice, and mites. A dull or dirty coat means something may be wrong. Bald or bare patches of skin showing through may be indications of ringworm or mange. A healthy coat should be full, possibly plush, glossy, soft and pleasant to touch or smell.

The eyes should be free of liquid discharge. Healthy eyes are clear with little or no excessive wetting. Look for abnormalities such as soreness, redness, or swelling. Be aware that a blue-eyed kitten with a solid white coat may be deaf.

A healthy kitten's nose should be cool and only slightly damp. If there is a liquid discharge from the nostrils, the kitten may have an infection. Sneezing, coughing, and runny nose could all be signs of upper respiratory infections, which can become serious and even life-threatening.

Examine the ears for abnormal discharge, dirt, or unpleasant odors. If a kitten constantly shakes its head and rubs its ears with its paws, look inside the ears. If you see a dark, waxlike substance, the kitten has ear mites, which are near-microscopic parasites that must be treated by a veterinarian. Mites create itching, which can lead to self-inflicted damage to the skin from the kitten's intense need to scratch.

Evaluating a Kitten's Personality

The best way to evaluate a kitten is to see it with its litter. Observe how it interacts with the others. A shy, nervous kitten is adorable and heartrending but can become quite a problem as a full-grown cat. Shy behavior may also be a manifestation of poor health.

The opposite problem is overaggressiveness. A litter of kittens, especially past six weeks of age, plays rough-and-tumble games like those of baby lions. However, now and again there is a tough guy who goes well beyond the limits of exuberant play and displays hostile and potentially dangerous behavior. It is not too difficult to distinguish play fighting from the real thing. Watch for a sullen facial expression, stiffened body, straight legs, arched back, contracted pupils of the eyes, and ears flattened against the side of the head. A kitten with these characteristics can be dangerous to other members of the litter and even to humans. A real cat bite is painful. Observe how such a kitten deals with its littermates, and project that behavior onto a fully grown cat. It may be best to avoid this little tough guy if you have small children or limited patience.

Look for typical, normal kitten behavior. When you see a kitten that you like, that seems to behave like a normal, happy youngster, ask the breeder to bring it to you for examination. If the kitten is not frightened, you're off to a good start. Hold the kitten up and examine its physical condition. A healthy-looking, clean, lively, alert kitten that does not seem to be nervous when you hold it is exactly the sort of pet to choose if you have young children or limited time to train your kitten.

Kitten Temperament

There are a number of behavior characteristics in cats and kittens, and they are typical of many breeds and nonbreeds alike. You may loosely refer to these characteristics as temperament types, but remember that these are informal conclusions drawn from practical experience and the experience of feline experts.

One of the most challenging aspects of getting a kitten is determining its temperament or personality traits. The belief that all cats are alike is a misconception. They are not. The differences may seem obscure to those who have little or no experience, but cats and kittens are distinct from one an-

other both individually and as breeds. See Chapter Three, "Breeds of Distinction," to see just how different the breeds are from one another. Of course, we are all at a disadvantage when trying to predict a kitten's personality or temperament type without knowing the characteristics of its breed and viewing its parents. What does help is artificially establishing general temperament types for all cats, both pedigreed and nonbreed.

Although all wild and domestic cats share a common set of basic behaviors and instincts (see Chapter Six, "Basic Cat Behavior"), there are a number of ways in which various cats express their own unique, instinctive actions and responses. These can easily be divided into temperament categories, useful for evaluating a kitten or adult cat. Do not be surprised, though, if a given cat shows more than one of the following temperament traits. There is always one aspect of a cat's traits that is more dominant than the others; that aspect is what determines its temperament category.

Assertive Type

Cats with assertive temperaments are characterized by their lack of self-doubt. It never occurs to such cats that you might actually say no to them about anything. They insist on waking you out of a sound sleep in the morning so that you can feed them, and they will not accept the idea of a closed door when they want to see various members of their family.

As kittens and young adults they are very playful and do everything in their power to get people to indulge their spirited moods. They are quite controlling of all things in their world. As kittens they are quite frisky, a trait that certainly carries over into adulthood. They will respond to the slightest attention paid, even a casual glance. Part of their charm is their assumption that everyone loves and admires them. Assertive cats are not the least bit frightened of any new person or situation. Among the generally assertive breeds are the American Shorthair, Manx, and Japanese Bobtail.

Cool Type

The cool cat is almost always calm and laid back. It is not lazy or bored. It is not even tired. It is simply at peace with its environment and usually too large a cat to go running around. Such cats enjoy the attention they receive from humans who live with them. Cool cats allow the world to come to them, bringing affectionate offerings of things that taste good and a great deal of oohing and aahing. These are cats accustomed to being pampered as they accept the attention with aloofness, tolerance, and a hint of disdain. Although they do move around when it suits their wants and pleasures, they are usually found in the same place resting and sleeping. Some cool cats have a regal air about them, while others appear to be too distracted to care one way or the other about the attention or favors offered. They are grateful, however, to be allowed to sleep, nap, or just sit quietly and watch you. Typical breeds of this temperament type are Persian, Scottish Fold, Ragdoll, and Exotic.

Energetic Type

Energetic cats pace about like fidgety tigers and then suddenly race across the room like hunters in hot pursuit of their prey. People living with these feline hot rods usually have snagged threads and claw marks on their clothing from the leaps their pets make hopping onto them, using them as a sort of springboard to a higher place.

As kittens, these high-energy cats are easily distracted, excitable, and responsive to the slightest attention given to them, unless they are investigating an unfamiliar sound or movement. They usually know their name and come running at the sound of it, or at least turn and look. Energetic types are rarely afraid of anything, are usually quite friendly, and move like lightning. Most of them are highly trainable. Among breeds of this temperament type are the Abyssinian, Somali, and Devon Rex.

Demonstrative Type

Of all the breeds, the Siamese best shows all of the traits of the demonstrative personality. Cats of this type are very demanding and will follow you around like a persistent dog, all the while "talking" to you in an endless stream of demands, pleas, and expressions of approval and disapproval. Such cats are very intelligent and friendly, but that does not stop them from delivering a torrent of vociferous complaints once you have returned from leaving them alone for a while.

Demonstrative types are extroverts and do not censor or

modify the expression of their feelings, their needs, or their desires. When they are in the mood for playing, they insist on being the center of attention. They cannot bear being ignored and go to great lengths to get the attention they crave so much. Conversely, they can be moody and shift from being affectionate to being downright annoying. In this context they may leap from the floor to the top of a cabinet, easily open cupboard doors and refrigerators with their paws, and meow constantly until they get what they are after.

Demonstrative cats are unpredictable. Your watching television or talking on the phone—in short, your not paying attention—is often treated as a violation of the contract between cat and owner. Despite all this, they are affectionate, fascinating, and totally devoted to their human families or fellow cats. Most breeds that in any way resemble the Siamese are like this.

Timid Type

This behavior is uncharacteristic of any breed or nonbreed cat. Still, it does appear within individual cats.

A timid cat is usually comfortable with its own family and in its own home. However, when strangers enter the house, its reaction can range from timidity to fear, whether the strangers are people, dogs, or other cats. Every time a timid cat must adjust to a new person or a new situation, it will disappear under a bed, into a closet, or behind a couch. It will hide as best it can until the "threat" has passed. In this situation, timidity turns to anxiety that the cat may express by not using its litter pan to relieve itself.

The issues underlying a timid personality are a lack of self-confidence and a feeling of danger. A timid cat may eventually investigate the new person cautiously or simply hide and wait for the intrusion to end. Such cats are either reserved, overly sensitive, bashful, suspicious, distrustful, or frightened. If a timid cat becomes frightened enough, it may try to defend itself by hissing, scratching, or even biting. They are easily scared and must be given every consideration and kindness. A loving cat person must never be overbearing with a timid cat but must handle it with gentleness and sensitivity.

Aggressive Type

Some kittens display aggressive behavior that may or may not develop further in adult life. Most aggressive kittens settle down as they mature. It is important to understand, however, that an aggressive cat can be a very unpleasant pet.

Aggressive behavior in kittens shows itself as hostile-seeming playfulness, unrelenting curiosity (not necessarily a bad trait), and irritating pushiness with people or littermates. In adult cats aggressive behavior takes the form of threatening conduct, stalking that may or may not conclude in pouncing, and perhaps an attack on another pet or human. It is an exaggeration of hunting maneuvers, the defense of territory, a challenge for higher social status or even for sexual rights. An aggressive cat may be endearing to its owner but frightening to all others, especially children.

Aggressive behavior can include holding a human's hand or wrist between the teeth when being stroked or petted (they rarely bite down), staring at you without flinching, raising hackles and standing directly in front of you in a crouched position, hissing and growling. An aggressive cat or kitten may scratch or bite when being petted or rubbed affectionately. So-called love bites are indicative of an aggressive type and call for caution.

It is best to avoid selecting a kitten or cat in which such

behaviors are clear and present. The aggressive type at best can be upsetting and at worst threatening or even dangerous. Such a cat or kitten may bite you accidentally or do it on purpose. Either way, it must either be avoided or dealt with quickly and firmly. See Chapter Ten, "The Short and Sweet Problem Solver."

Where to Get a Kitten

It seems that cats and kittens are everywhere. Although this is not quite true, there is an abundance of cats and kittens and it's very easy to find one. Like it or not, there is no shortage. Taking a free kitten from a neighbor or from an ad in the local paper may seem like a good idea but is not necessarily the best way. There are many unknown factors in such situations. Where you get your cat matters.

Adoption

There are large numbers of people involved in rescuing abandoned and lost cats and dogs. Sometimes they are known in a community by reputation and sometimes they advertise in local newspapers, offering cats for little or no money. All you have to do is show them that you can provide a good home with loving care. These well-intentioned people do this work on their own without thought of recognition or profit. The fact is, whether one approves of them or not, they rescue otherwise doomed cats and dogs, give them medical attention, alter them, feed them, clean them up, and place them in proper homes. If you are fortunate enough to find such a person or persons in your community, it is a fine way to acquire a kitten. Just be sure that the pet you receive enjoys a clean bill of health from a vet.

A more traditional method of adoption is through a community animal shelter or an SPCA-type organization. This is still a good bargain when it comes to buying a kitten or a grown cat. The animal will likely be in reasonably good health. If the kitten is too young for neutering when you get it, the organization requires that you agree to have the operation done at the proper time.

Most cats and kittens up for adoption are random-bred, but on occasion a purebred cat comes through. When considering acquiring a kitten, by all means check your Yellow Pages phone directory and look for "animal shelter" listings.

Breeders

The noncommercial or hobby breeder is usually quite knowledgeable, experienced, and caring about his or her cats and kittens. Most are part of the Cat Fancy (as the world of pedigreed cats is known) and maintain *catteries* with a number of breeding male and female cats. Breeders usually register their cats and kittens with an accepted cat organization such as the CFA (Cat Fanciers' Association). Although breaking even financially is an important consideration, more often pride in the quality of their cats and kittens is their true reward and motivation. Here, pedigreed cats of the most interesting and beautiful breeds are bred and brought into the world with the greatest selection and care possible. Each kitten is registered with one of the various cat registering organizations and is kept with its mother and litter for the proper length of time. A kitten is permitted to leave for a new home, provided the humans involved appear to be kind, thoughtful, and humane. These breeders also produce most of the brilliant cats seen in cat shows throughout the world. Noncommercial breeders are quite fussy about who gets their cats, despite the fact that their kittens are almost always quite expensive. Although there are a few unfortunate exceptions, this is how the large majority of breeders function.

The very best of the noncommercial breeders can be found by contacting any of the various cat registering organizations or by consulting ads in magazines that are exclusively about cats.

"Backyard breeders" are amateurs and, as such, should be approached with caution. Such breeders may have limited knowledge of actual breeding or technical skill and may not breed their cats selectively. And if they haven't taken certain health precautions, it's anyone's guess as to the soundness of the resulting kittens. Consequently, such breeders may set loose into the world even more kittens for which there are all-too-few homes. It is a risk at best and a detriment to the cause of reducing the tragic overpopulation of small animals.

Commercial breeders are often the source of kittens and puppies for pet shops, although they often place ads in local newspapers and sell animals directly to those shopping around. They usually breed in large quantities. Profit is the only consideration, which brings into serious question the true quality and health of the animals made available. Some commercial breeders are responsible in their activities and function fairly and competently. The trick is to figure out which ones.

You can still purchase some kittens at a pet shop, but this is no longer a common situation. A pet shop will sell both pedigreed and nonpedigreed kittens despite their availability from other sources. By charging lower prices for them, they hope to attract customers for the highly profitable cat supplies and paraphernalia.

The owners of some pet shops breed their own cats and

maintain them until they are sold. Most shops, however, obtain their kittens from local commercial breeders or from various commercial sources of questionable origin and quality. Kittens in pet shops may be of a specific breed (with or without registration papers from a cat association) or of no particular breed, which means they will not have papers indicating they have been registered with a cat association.

If you go to a pet shop to buy a kitten, look the shop over carefully. Be wary of salespeople who love nothing better than placing a kitten (or puppy) in your arms. They count on your having an emotional response and purchasing the kitten on impulse. This is all wrong. The hit-or-miss risk of getting a pet shop kitten is much the same as that involved in acquiring a pet from a backyard breeder. Let the buyer beware.

Believe it or not, veterinarians are indirectly (and sometimes directly) responsible for placing many kittens in new homes. In countless veterinary clinics and hospitals, there is a bulletin board littered with dozens of notices about homeless kittens and cats. Vets have traditionally served their communities and their clientele as a clearinghouse for those who must find new homes for their pets and those who are looking for pets. They are another great source to consider when looking for a new kitten.

Finally, there are those cats and kittens that seek you out and choose to be part of your family. It really happens. Like magic, some cats simply appear at your windowsill or doorway and walk right into your life, knocking over a flower arrangement and taking up residence in your umbrella stand. Lost or abandoned strays are sometimes lucky enough, or perceptive enough, to claim and adopt the right household. It does happen and is worth mentioning. It is, of course, your moral responsibility to try to find a stray cat's owner and home. If no owner can be found, consider yourself blessed. Cats that choose their owners can be particularly loyal and affectionate.

No matter how you finally got a kitten to move in with you, it is important to understand what you can expect in the coming years with the newest member of your family. Keep this handy reference by your side and use it.

There are those cats and kittens that seek you out
and choose to be part of your family.

THREE

BREEDS OF DISTINCTION: A THUMBNAIL GUIDE TO UNCOMMON CATS

The magnetic, pedigreed cats seen in competition at cat shows fascinate most cat lovers. Despite their sumptuous beauty and unique qualities, most of them live in the homes of their owners as household pets and they too are family cats. The Cat Fanciers' Association (CFA) has thus far accepted the forty-one breeds described here for registration and most of them for championship competition. Here then is a brief description of each one for your pleasure and future reference. Who knows, someday you may be intrigued enough to acquire such a kitten.

Pedigreed Cats Registered by the Cat Fanciers' Association (CFA)

Abyssinian	LaPerm
American Bobtail	Maine Coon Cat
American Curl	Manx
American Shorthair	Norwegian Forest Cat
American Wirehair	Ocicat
Balinese	Oriental
Birman	Persian
Bombay	RagaMuffin
British Shorthair	Ragdoll
Burmese	Russian Blue
Chartreux	Scottish Fold
Colorpoint Shorthair	Selkirk Rex
Cornish Rex	Siamese
Devon Rex	Siberian
Egyptian Mau	Singapura
European Burmese	Somali
Exotic	Sphynx
Havana Brown	Tonkinese
Japanese Bobtail	Turkish Angora
Javanese	Turkish Van
Korat	

Abyssinian. These unusual cats bear a remarkable resemblance to those in paintings and sculptures of ancient Egypt despite the fact that their origins are a subject of speculation and mystery. These elegant felines have broad chests, slim bodies, long legs, and large pointed ears and almond-shaped eyes. They are quite muscular. Their heads form a modified wedge.

The CFA accepts Abyssinians in four coat colors: ruddy,

red, blue, and fawn. The breed is best for those who will enjoy living with a spirited, affectionate, and extremely energetic companion. They are highly intelligent cats, very curious and quite athletic. Far from being lap cats, they present their human families with lightninglike starts and speedy runs around the house, like a souped-up sports car. When they require your attention, they are adept at getting it; they can be soft and fuzzy when they want affection but only on their own terms. When left alone with no one to play with, they will become bored and find new and interesting ways to get into trouble. It is best, especially for a kitten, to have a playmate in its new house.

American Bobtail. Well-named, the American Bobtail bears a striking resemblance to its wild namesake. Of course, this is where the resemblance ends: the domestic cat is smaller and has a gentle, loving temperament. Bobtails are medium-to-large cats with short tails, no two alike. The average length of the tail is one to four inches; however, some are shorter or longer. The cats are muscular and athletic. Their heads are modified wedge-shape, with a well-defined brow above their large, nearly almond-shaped eyes. Their unique coat comes in a short-haired variety with medium semidense hair and in a long-haired variety with semilong hair that is somewhat shaggy. The coat is resilient and resistant to water. You can show them in all colors and patterns.

Despite their wild look, American Bobtails have a sweet disposition and are very adaptive to living with a human family. These extremely intelligent cats have doglike personalities and are devoted to their families. They are well behaved and sensitive to those in distress, so much so that psychotherapists can use them in treatment programs. With their clownlike behavior, American Bobtails make excellent companions for children.

American Curl. The distinctive feature of this breed is the unusual formation of its ears, which curl back and form an arc. The ears are firm to the touch, erect, and open, curving gently. Breeders have bred these cats in long-haired and short-haired coats. The CFA allows them to be registered and to compete in the show ring in a wide array of colors in the solid, shaded, smoke, tabby, bi-color, parti-color, and pointed patterns. The first American Curl appeared spontaneously in 1981 on the doorsteps of Joe and Grace Ruga of Lakewood, California, where they adopted it and named it Shulamith. Selective breeding and presentation of these rare and highly unusual cats began in 1983. In 1991 CFA gave the breed provisional status and in 1993 accepted it for championship competition.

American Curls love to be with their human families, and they adjust to other pets, children, and new situations quickly. They are affectionate and very faithful. Experienced Curl people say the cats are very attentive to their families, constantly following them around. Although they are not overly talkative, they express their curiosity and intelligence with little chirping sounds rather than the customary meow. American Curls seem to hold on to their kittenlike personalities throughout their lives and can be quite playful into old age.

American Shorthair. Although this breed is descended from basic European working cats that arrived in North America with the earliest settlers, their devoted admirers consider them to be among the few truly American cat breeds. They are called "working cats" because of their great hunting skills. They are often mistaken for the basic, nonpedigreed house cats that they resemble in body type and shape. The difference between the mixed-breed house cat and the pedigreed American Shorthair becomes obvious after a careful examination of the two. Since 1904 devoted Shorthair breeders have been selectively breeding with great success the best examples for their physical and mental excellence. The difference between them and their unpedigreed relatives stems from the many generations of careful development by breeders to meet specific, demanding breed standards set forth by a number of cat registering organizations including CFA. These standards dictate size, type, shape, colors, and coat patterns.

American Shorthairs are strong, muscular, intelligent, lively cats and are athletic, sweet-natured, independent, and highly dignified. They present the look of a strongly built, well-balanced, and symmetrical cat with conformation indicating power, endurance, and agility. American Shorthairs are striking to look at and yet seem to represent all cats everywhere. Those interested can register them with the CFA in a wide array of colors in the solid, shaded, smoke, tabby, parti-color, and bi-color patterns.

American Wirehair. The unique wiry-looking coat is this breed's most distinctive feature, although there is considerable variation in its texture and length from cat to cat. Each hair is hooked or crimped, giving the cat a woolly appearance. The coat, which is not only springy, dense, and resilient but also coarse and hard to the touch, distinguishes the American Wirehair from all other breeds. The coat comes in different degrees of wiriness: it can be soft and woolly like terry cloth or fine and sparse with a varied range of textures and densities. This entire breed can be traced to one cat, named Adam, who was a spontaneous mutation in a litter in Verona, New York, in 1966. He was born with fur more like sheep wool than the traditional coats of his non-pedigreed parents.

Since that time, the American Wirehair has become an

original American breed and bred to type. They are active cats, agile, with a great curiosity about their surroundings. They are clever enough to open cabinet doors and even some full-size doors with their paws. Wirehairs enjoy playing with children, dogs, cats, and most other animals. Those who live with these wiry cats, which are similar in body type to American Shorthairs, say they are easy to care for, are resistant to disease, and make wonderful companions. CFA allows them to be shown in a wide array of colors.

Balinese. The Balinese is an American-created breed but with a distinctly Siamese background. In the early sixties they were considered mutated long-haired Siamese. They are now a recognized breed in their own right. Still, they have not lost the gregarious Siamese character and talkative inclination. Named after the graceful dancers of Bali, they are only permitted the four traditional point colors★ of the Siamese: seal point, chocolate point, blue point, and lilac point. Their luxurious coat is of medium-length, fine, silky without a downy undercoat lying close to the body. It may appear to be shorter than it is. The hair is longest on the tail, which is similar in structure to the Siamese tail except for the hair spreading out into a sumptuous plume.

The personalities of Balinese are similar to those of all Siamese cats. They are very vocal and demand human attention. These are good-natured cats with an unquenchable curiosity. They insist on participating in all human activities such as reading, writing, and sitting on the couch with you. The Balinese is an active creature that is intelligent and loving.

★Refers to a coat pattern involving a darker color on body extremities than appears on the major portion of the torso. Points include the face, ears, feet, and tail. The Siamese is typical of this pattern.

Birman. Their beautiful blue eyes and luxurious coat and color combinations create the false impression that these are simply Siamese cats with a posh coat. Upon careful examination, one soon discovers that they are a separate, distinctive colorpointed cat breed (which means they have a darker color on their tail, legs, ears, and face). The Birman is a unique, natural cat distinguished by the *white gloves* at the end of all four paws. In more recent times it has been permitted with many more point colors than the original four restricted to Siamese. The unique white color that runs from the feet up the back of the hind legs seems to intrigue most spectators at cat shows. They are referred to as *gloves* and *laces*. The body must be long and stocky with medium-length heavy legs, large round paws, and a medium-length tail. The eyes are deep blue and almost round. They are seen in the original four point colors—seal point, blue point, chocolate point, lilac point—but are also allowed a variety of colors in solid point, lynx point, and parti-color point. All Birmans, of course, must have the distinctive white gloves on each of their four paws.

The Birman personality is as engaging as its sumptuous appearance. These cats are gentle, active, and playful but quite often quiet and subdued. They are loving animals that prefer to sit with you or sleep on your lap than to run around like the more active breeds. They are soft-spoken cats until they require your attention, and at times they do demand attention.

Bombay. Cat lovers can only see the glistening coat of the Bombay in solid jet black, contrasted by its glimmering copper or gold eyes. Resembling a panther, this hybrid breed is the result of crossing a black American Shorthair to a sable Burmese. After years of selective breeding, the cats finally bred true, thanks exclusively to the arduous efforts of breeder Nikki Horner of Louisville, Kentucky. Creating the breed in the fifties in America, she named it for the black leopards of India. These highly unusual cats are not simply black cats. Part of what makes them unique is their distinctive head shape, body type, and adherence to the specific breed standard set forth by the CFA and other cat registering organizations. They are medium-size cats, bearing little resemblance to their foundation breeds, the American Shorthair and the Burmese. The Bombay is seen exclusively with a jet-black coat.

Bombays are friendly cats, playful, soft-spoken, and very affectionate. Great companion animals, they enjoy the company of humans for hours on end. They love to follow you whenever you move and wherever you go just like dogs. These intelligent cats are easy to train for the basics, love to play, and are quite adaptive to other animals and children as well. Although not overly active, they are personable and not at all shy.

British Shorthair. These compelling "Brits" are not commonly seen in the United States, but their distinctive look commands much attention and admiration at cat shows. They are possibly the oldest English cat breed, one whose roots go back to the streets of ancient Rome. They are large, powerful-looking cats, compact with a good depth of body, a full broad chest, short- to medium-length strong legs, with a round head. Their coat is short and dense. After World War I, Persians were introduced to the breed, along with selected domestic shorthairs, to create the plush, sophisticated cat seen today. (It is a practice that is no longer allowed by any cat registering body.) They are seen in a wide array of colors in the solid, shaded, smoke, tabby, parti-color, and bi-color patterns.

These friendly cats have a quiet sense of dignity often

mistaken for aloofness. The most pleasing aspect of the British Shorthair personality is its gentleness. They are easygoing, good-natured, and highly intelligent. Possibly because of their large size, they are not fast or athletic and prefer being on the ground rather than jumping to high places. They are fine companions and loving family cats.

Burmese. The eyes of the Burmese are rounded pools of liquid gold, open wide and softly concentrated as they stare at you with unreserved curiosity. Their round heads blend into compact, curvy bodies, a substantial bone structure and well-developed muscles hidden under a blanket of silk. Their heft comes as a surprise when you lift one. The overall impression of the ideal Burmese is a cat of medium size seen in rich solid colors with expressive eyes and a sweet facial expression. The Burmese coat comes in four colors: sable, champagne, blue, and platinum.

These are soft-spoken, active cats with a pleasing personality. They are playful cats with a lot of funny moves, from quick rollovers to prancing back and forth. They are quite social and enjoy the company of humans. Affection is always returned freely and generously.

Chartreux (pronounced shar trew). These ancient cats are large, strapping felines with woolly double coats, which are thought to have evolved in order to insulate them from the harsh weather of Asia Minor's mountainous terrain, where by some accounts they originated. True lovers of the breed covet them for their hunting prowess and their dense, water-repellent fur. Its husky, robust type is sometimes termed primitive, neither broad chested nor tubular shaped. Though amply built, Chartreux are extremely supple and agile cats—refined, never coarse or clumsy. They apparently existed long before they came to live with the Carthusian monks in their motherhouse, Le Grand Chartreux, circa the sixteenth century. The modern Chartreux color is any shade of blue-gray from ash to slate with an emphasis on clarity and uniformity rather than shade. The preferred tone is a bright, unblemished blue with an overall iridescent sheen.

These cats are expert climbers enabled by their powerful bodies and muscular hind legs. Among the most skilled animal hunters, they are expert at catching mice. Nevertheless, they are friendly and quite amiable with most humans, especially members of the family, but also with other pets and visitors. They are well-behaved pets and speak in almost inaudible meows. They are almost as silent as the monks of Chartreux.

Colorpoint Shorthair. The Colorpoint Shorthair appears to be a Siamese but with colors other than the traditional Siamese point colors (seal, chocolate, blue, and lilac). CFA accepts the Colorpoint Shorthair as a separate breed, partly because traditional Siamese breeders do not wish to permit any colors other than the four traditional ones and partly because they were crossed with American Shorthairs to introduce the new colors. (Complicating the issue further is the Oriental breed, another nontraditional version of the Siamese. It does not have color points at all on the extremities of its body but rather an overall solid coat color.)

According to its CFA Breed Standard, "The Colorpoint Shorthair is a medium sized, svelte, refined cat with long tapering lines, very lithe, but muscular. Males may be proportionately larger. The ideal is a cat with type identical to the Siamese, but with its own distinct and unique colors." These cats have vivid blue eyes that are almond-shaped and set in a long, tapering wedge-shaped head. CFA permits them in a variety of colors in solid and lynx points (stripes).

Similar in personality to the Siamese, these are intelligent cats with an affectionate nature and a desire for human companionship. Show cats or pets, these beauties are doglike in their desire to do tricks such as fetch, to talk to you as much as possible, and to follow you around your house. They are active cats, extremely inquisitive, and quite athletic. They are graceful, elegant, and very playful.

Cornish Rex. The most distinguishing feature of this unusual breed is a soft, wavy, downlike coat covering a delicate, tubular body referred to in its Breed Standard as "racy." The coat has no guard hairs or topcoat, which exaggerates the cat's large, erect ears and wide-open facial features. (Guard hairs are coarse, thick straight hairs that taper to a fine point and are usually part of the outer coat.) The breed's comparatively small, egg-shaped head presents high cheekbones, hollow cheeks, and a high-bridged Roman nose. Its extreme look is perfect for those who desire an unusual-looking cat. Small to medium in size and lean, the Cornish Rex is the result of a spontaneous mutation born to domestic shorthairs during the 1950s. There are two recessive Rex genes, the Cornish and the Devon, that cannot breed together to produce a Rex cat. Both genes cause the cat to have a curly undercoat with no topcoat. On close examination the obvious difference between the two breeds lies in their coats. The Devon coat has a fuller feeling and a more open and uneven wave, completely unlike the Marcel wave of the Cornish Rex coat, which has no guard hairs at all.

In many ways, the personality of the Cornish Rex and its close cousin, the Devon Rex, resembles the personality of the Siamese. It is an intensely curious cat, affectionate, needful of human attention, and highly talkative. It is very playful.

Devon Rex. The Devon first appeared in Devon, England, as a spontaneous mutation ten years after the Cornish Rex first appeared. Genetically, the Devon Rex is a completely separate breed from the Cornish Rex despite their similarities and all cat-registering bodies present them as such. The reason is abundantly clear after casual observation. The Devon's wide-open, all-consuming eyes, its large bat-wing ears, and its innocent face, concealing a mischief-making sprite, is the focus for those who see the breed for the first time—that and its unusual Rex coat. The Rex coat of the Devon, the reason for its recognition as a breed, is somewhat fuller than the coat of its cousin, the Cornish. This is because the Devon has guard hairs, although fewer than other breeds, of varying length and thickness, which create a slightly more ample feeling to the coat and a more open and uneven wave unlike the Marcel wave of the Cornish Rex coat, which does not have guard hairs. (Guard hairs are coarse, thick straight hairs that taper to a fine point and are usually part of the outer coat.) The CFA Breed Standard says of its waviness; "A rippled wave effect should be apparent when the coat is smoothed with one's hand. The wave is most evident where the coat is the longest, on the body and tail." The Devon is a small-to-medium sized cat with long legs adding a rakish appearance. CFA permits a wide array of coat colors in the solid, shaded, smoke, tabby, bi-color, and pointed patterns.

The Devon Rex personality is similar to the Siamese. The Devon is a blithe spirit of a cat, alert and active showing a lively interest in everything in and outside its home. It is friendly, charming, and often comical. It will follow you around the house, react to its name, and enjoy cuddling in bed with you. Perhaps because of its less dense coat, it craves the warmth of the human body. It can completely flatter a stranger by jumping into his or her lap without any introduction.

Many Devon breeders are convinced that because of the

breed's low shedding, it is ideal for those suffering with cat-related allergies. They believe that the pleasure of living with a Devon is a real possibility for those so afflicted. Although there is no scientific evidence for this assertion, there are a number of Devon owners who claim to know it is true from their experience.

Egyptian Mau. The Mau retains a hint of its wild ancestors, as do all domestic cats to a lesser degree, if you accept the suggestion of their origins from ancient Egyptian cats. It is the only natural domesticated breed with a fully spotted coat, like a homegrown leopard or cheetah in miniature. Sleek and muscular, its long legs (the hind legs being longer) give it the capability of great bursts of speed and high leaps reminiscent of the cheetah. It even has a cheetahlike gait, which creates the impression that it walks on tiptoes. Its physical appearance strikes a delicate balance between the compactness of a Burmese and the slim elegance of a Siamese. With light "gooseberry green" eyes, these cats are randomly spotted and allowed by CFA to be shown in three coat colors: silver, bronze, and smoke.

The Egyptian Mau personality varies from cat to cat, between aloofness and sociability. Generally, they are affectionate with their own families but reserved with strangers, conforming to the myth that cats' typical behavior is aloof reserve. They make close friends with only a special few. It is a fact, however, that given time they warm up to most considerate strangers. Like its cousin, the more active Abyssinian, the Egyptian Mau has a birdlike vocal quality that is both soft and mellow.

European Burmese. According to the CFA breed description, the European Burmese "is the CFA name for the ten-color Burmese breed developed outside North America. The name reflects the breed's origin and marks it as a different CFA breed than the round, compact, four-color Burmese breed. Besides having six more colors, the European Burmese are moderate, gently rounded cats with a longer body and head.

"With their luminous eyes and striking colors, the European Burmese are exceptionally beautiful. Up close, their silky, close-lying coat and harmonious conformation become more evident. These cats are medium in size and length, with a solid, hefty body and remarkable yellow to amber eyes."

Their coats are satinlike in texture with almost no undercoat. European Burmese solid and tortoiseshell colors are brown, blue, chocolate, lilac, red, cream, brown tortie, blue tortie, chocolate tortie, and lilac tortie.*

These are endearing cats with expressive eyes and a sweet facial expression. Like the Burmese, European Burmese are affectionate, intelligent cats and enjoy the company of other animals; however, they live quite happily as an only pet. They are calm, friendly, and comfortable both at home and in the show ring. They are elegant and unique.

Exotic. The Exotic looks like a Persian with a summer clip. However, the medium length, plush coat is not the result of an appointment with a grooming salon but rather the result of selective breeding. Exotics are identical to Persians in every respect except for coat length. Several California breeders began the creation of this breed in the early 1960s by crossing Persians with American Shorthairs. Initially, those involved did not intend to create a new breed but were more interested in the look of a Persian with a short coat.

---

*"Tortie" refers to a tortoiseshell coat, black with random patches of red.

CFA officially recognized this hybrid breed in 1966. The result is that you can have the massive, heavy-boned look of a Persian along with a low-maintenance coat that does not resemble the coat of any other shorthaired cat. Exotics' large, round eyes are set wide apart in a large, round head. Their thick, plush coat softens the lines of the cat and accentuates the roundness of their appearance. CFA allows a wide array of colors in the solid, shaded, smoke, tabby, bi-color, and pointed patterns.

Despite their size and cautious behavior with strangers, Exotics are friendly, outgoing cats and quite charming. These are gentle members of the family with a sharp wit to go with their plush coats. Exotics have a sweet disposition and a talent for finding the best places to lounge around the house. They are quiet, docile, and affectionate. Like Persians, they are delightful cats.

Havana Brown. The only relation these sumptuous cats have to the city of Havana is the solid dark color of their coats. Their coats come in a deep mahogany brown tobacco, down to the roots, like fine cigars. Even the whiskers are brown. The coat is of medium length, smooth and lustrous. This hybrid breed is the result of long and complex reproduction efforts involving, over the years, the crossbreeding of many different cats, including Siamese, Russian Blues, and black domestic shorthairs, to create the delicious brown coat and unique body type, which bears no resemblance to any other breed. Its body is of medium length and structure, not tubular like the Siamese or broad chested like the American Shorthair. The Havana Brown is only recognized in this solid brown color by CFA.

This bright, active cat reminds one of a Burmese until closer examination. It is a sweet and loving cat that draws much of its personality from the best of the breeds that were combined to create it. Its voice is soft and captivating, and it loves to express its curiosity with its paws rather than with its nose, as is the case with other breeds. The Havana Brown is highly social, affectionate, intelligent, and quite playful.

Japanese Bobtail. The Japanese Bobtail is a natural cat breed that originated in Japan. Its name comes from the unique look of its tail, which is short and much like a bunny's bobtail. Rounded tufts of fur mask the tail's bone structure, formed by curves, angles, kinks, or any combination of these. The Bobtail is a medium-sized cat with a long, lean, and elegant torso. There is no inclination toward flabbiness, a broad chest or a thick torso. CFA allows the Japanese Bobtail two varieties, short-haired and long-haired. The short-haired coat is medium in length. The long-haired coat is medium-to-long in length. It has no noticeable undercoat. CFA permits the Bobtail in a wide array of colors in the solid, tabby, parti-color, and bi-color patterns and in some colors with the addition of white. However, like those depicted in ancient Japanese art, the much-preferred coats are the flashy spotted bi-colors and van bi-colors (predominantly white coats with color found only on the head and tail with occasional spots on the legs). The *mi-ke* (pronounced *mee-kay*) or calico was once the most prized color.

Like delicate geishas, Japanese Bobtails discreetly enter a room and liven it with their slightly slanted eyes, high cheekbones, and bright, cheerful coats. The Bobtail personality is somewhat serious, with random spurts of playfulness. They are active cats that always seem to be busy going somewhere or doing something. They are devoted family pets that love you but from a bit of a distance. They are congenial, highly intelligent companions, clever enough to open cabinet doors, curious enough to rummage through the contents. The Japanese Bobtail is a lively, spirited cat filled with mischief and the desire to play.

Javanese. Although registered as a separate breed by CFA, the Javanese is a long-haired Siamese—but with a significant difference. Unlike its close relative, the Balinese, which is also a long-haired version of the Siamese, CFA allows the Javanese in a wide variety of coat colors in solid point, lynx point, and parti-color point. Interestingly, CFA does not allow the Javanese in championship competition in the four traditional Siamese point colors. So essentially, the Javanese is the long-haired Siamese in a wide variety of coat colors other than those seen in the Siamese and the Balinese.

Its body type is foreign (like the Siamese), svelte with long tapering lines, strong and muscular. It has fine bones and firm muscles. The coat type is medium to long, fine, silky with no downy undercoat.

Javanese personalities are similar to those of all Siamese and Balinese cats. They are very demanding of human attention. These are good-natured cats, loving, with an unquenchable curiosity. They insist on participating in all family activities. They are playful yet refined. They are talkative but very elegant.

Korat. The Korat is an ancient, natural breed from the Korat province of Thailand. Its only coat color is silver-tipped blue. Thai people describe this color as "rain-cloud gray," and its silvering effect as "sea foam." The silver tips create a shimmering look as the cat moves. The CFA official standard accepts no other coat color. It is a medium-sized cat characterized by its semicobby body (not long and lean like a Siamese, or short like a Manx, but with a tapered waist and medium bone structure). Its head is heart-shaped and it has a single coat with short, fine, glossy hairs lying close to the body. It is heavier than it appears.

The Korat is not very talkative and has soft vocalizations. It will respond playfully to human attention and is very

friendly. Family life is much to its liking, and strong relationships develop quickly. This intelligent feline enjoys its many
naps throughout the day, although it is keenly aware of
everything in its surroundings. Korats are alert and attentive
and listen to everything going on. The Thai people consider
them good luck.

LaPerm. The name refers to the breed's wavy or curly hair, its
major trait. LaPerm is one of the newer CFA breeds accepted
for registration. It is unique because of its unusual-looking
coat, which is not only wavy or curly but appears in both
longhair and shorthair. The cat is medium-sized and of what
is called a semiforeign type, which means svelte, and fine-
boned with tapered lines. The head shape resembles a modified wedge with rounded contours. A good example of the
breed will have a moderately soft, springy coat texture standing away from the body in ringlet curls or waves over most of
the cat; the curlier the better. Only the long-haired version
has a neck ruff (similar to a lion's mane) and a curly plumed
tail. All colors and coat patterns are acceptable to CFA.

These are gentle and affectionate cats yet quite active.
They can change in an instant from extreme activity to quiet
meditation on your lap. They enjoy the company of humans
and let you know it the minute they see you. You can hold
them, drape them over your shoulder, or cradle them in your
arms. You'll get no complaints.

The first kitten of this breed occurred spontaneously as a
natural mutation in 1982 in The Dalles, Oregon. CFA accepted the breed for registration in the miscellaneous class
in 2000. The LaPerm garners a great deal of public attention
at cat shows.

Maine Coon Cat. This true American cat breed is impressive
in every way. Its transition from large, wild-looking rural cat

to glamorous show cat is nothing short of amazing. Despite its time-honored brown tabby coat with black rings on its big bushy tail, no domestic cat ever mated with a raccoon to create it, as some people believe. The Maine Coon Cat has a medium-to-large, muscular, broad-chested body covered with a heavy, shaggy coat that is silky and falls smoothly. CFA permits a wide array of colors in the solid, shaded, smoke, tabby, bi-color, and parti-color patterns. Some cat fanciers believe it is the largest of all the pedigreed cats.

The Maine Coon Cat has a pleasing personality consisting of self-confidence, assertiveness, and calm playfulness. It adjusts easily to other cats and even some dogs with ease and comfort but tends to dominate most situations. Despite its slight voice, it is a formidable hunter. The Maine Coon Cat is a natural breed and is considered to be a native American.

Manx. Originating from the Isle of Man, situated in the Irish Sea between England and Ireland, these unusual cats are believed to have appeared hundreds of years ago. What sets them apart from all other cats is their lack of a tail, their back legs being much longer than their forelegs, and their magnetic, rounded, yet slightly slanted eyes. Although the perfect show Manx has no tail whatsoever, some appear with one or two tail vertebrae. Breeders and cat show people call this very short riser-type tail a *stubby.* Those born with a full-length tail are called a *longie* and the tailless Manx is called a *rumpy,* which is the only type accepted for show. They present a rounded appearance in terms of their heads, cheeks, and hindquarters. They may have short-haired or long-haired coats. Both coat lengths are plush with a luxurious downy undercoat. CFA permits Manx to be shown in a wide array of colors in the solid, shaded, smoke, tabby, bi-color, and parti-color patterns.

The Manx is an energetic cat with a distinctive personality that is born out of its great intelligence. It is extremely playful, stubborn, and a bit of a mischief maker. No empty box, bag, or bowl is safe from its four-legged jump. These cats are competent hunters and some even like to swim as well as retrieve. Most tend to get along with dogs quite well, but their main interest is the human family. They become very devoted, especially to children. Their voices are soft, low, and chirpy. They are extremely lovable creatures.

Norwegian Forest Cat (Norsk Skogkatt). These are hardy cats with a keen appreciation for open spaces and independence. Lovingly called the *wegie* (*wee gee*) by their devotees, they are sometimes mistaken for Maine Coon Cats because of their large size and profuse double coats (with long, glossy, and smooth water-resistant fur on top), broad chests, and muscular bodies. They are moderate in length, with males larger and more imposing than females. Their back legs are longer than their front legs, making their rump higher than their shoulders, which distinguishes them from the Maine Coon Cat. However, it is their profuse, flowing coats that attract so much attention, that and their sweet facial expression and bright eyes. The thickness of their coat varies with the season—less undercoat in warm weather, more in cold weather. In the summer, the cat's bushy tail may be the only indication that it is a longhair. CFA allows a wide array of coat colors in the solid, shaded, smoke, parti-color, and bi-color patterns.

Although wegies love a certain amount of freedom and independence, they accept domestic life rather well. They do enjoy climbing trees, given the opportunity, and because of their strong legs can climb down headfirst. Norwegian Forest Cats like human company but they are cautious with strangers. Wegies are sociable with everyone in their families but often become more attached to one person. They are intelligent felines with a fabulous hunting skill. They adjust well to new homes, other pets, and children. Not known as lap cats, they do enjoy expressions of affection, but only when they choose. They are usually quite calm but can often be stirred into action if the stimulus is the right one, such as food, play, or something to hunt. They are good companions.

Ocicat. More than any other domestic cat, the Ocicat resembles a large wild cat. Its suggestion of wildness at first startles spectators at cat shows: its spotted coat suggests a similarity to the ocelot, a spotted, leopardlike cat native to the southwestern United States. If you did not know better, you would think it was something ferocious, better off in a zoo. However, this hybrid breed was created by crossing Siamese and Abyssinian cats, in a setting far removed from mountains, jungles, and deserts. The Ocicat is a medium-to-large feline of considerable strength and of a moderate body type. It possesses a solid, long-bodied torso, with substantial bone and muscle development. It is always a spotted cat with tipped or *agouti* fur (each hair has bands of color). A spot is formed where the agouti hairs fall together. The striking contrast between these spots and the background color account for its wild-animal appeal to the public. The Ocicat is bred for many colors; darker spots appearing on a lighter background create its "wildcat" appearance.

Although there is nothing dangerous about these very sweet domestic cats, they are alert to their surroundings and show great vitality. They are friendly and gentle, as are all domesticated cats. Their primary activities are napping and "talking" to their family. They are not demanding but are totally devoted cats.

Oriental. The Oriental's reason for being is its coat color, whether it is solid, shaded, smoke, parti-color, bi-color, or tabby-patterned. Orientals originated in England in the 1950s with breeders who wanted a Siamese cat with a *self-colored* (solid-color) coat. The Siamese breeders on both sides of the Atlantic were then and continue to be unyielding in their insistence on the Siamese's being a pointed cat with the four classic point colors: seal, chocolate, blue, and lilac. The Oriental (originally named the Oriental Shorthair) is a hybrid breed created by crossing the Siamese with various shorthairs and later with longhairs by those who wanted a Siamese-type cat that was not pointed. With this breed, you may choose a Siamese-type cat from one of over three hundred colors and coat patterns in addition to choosing either a longhair or a shorthair variety.

The personality of this breed is similar to that of the Siamese, including its very talkative nature and desire to stick close to you. Still, there may be traces of the behavior of those cats used originally to create the breed, such as the Russian Blue and various solid-color shorthairs. They are assertive and outgoing cats, great attention getters.

Persian. Of all the unusual and exquisite beauties seen at a cat show, none commands attention like the Persian. Cat lovers never tire of ogling this sovereign breed as it sits majestically staring with regal indifference. Its luxurious long hair is combed and brushed, puffed and primped for show ring competition like an expensive couch ornament. Persians are allowed to be bred in a wide variety of coat colors in the solid, shaded, smoke, tabby, bi-color, parti-color, and pointed patterns. Under all the fluff, however, is a short, stocky body with heavily boned legs and a deep, broad chest. Besides their long, beautiful coats, their eyes enrapture everyone. They are large, colorful pools of liquid, round and compelling. Getting a Persian to look at you is the equivalent of catching a fly ball at a Major League Baseball game. You have to earn that privilege.

The origin of this breed remains an unsolved mystery in the cat world. Many experts believe it came from Turkey, Persia (Iran), or India. This is quite likely. Although Persians are an ancient natural breed, registering organizations consider them modern cats because they have been modified by highly selective breeding efforts begun in the late nineteenth century.

Although they give the appearance of being docile, sitting with their front legs tucked under, Persians constantly demand the attention of their loved ones and can be quite insistent. They are not dainty or agile and do not like to climb or jump to high places like other cats. They are posers as they drape themselves like furry doilies on a soft chair or sunny windowsill. They are responsive to those who love them, play with them, and pay attention. They are very affectionate, with the right person.

RagaMuffin. This massive teddy bear of a cat is docile yet alert to all that is going on within its own view. Its large, walnut-shaped eyes are wide puddles of magnetic fixation. They are the feature that most often draws a person to this heavy-boned cat. RagaMuffins are bred in all coat colors and patterns, with pointed and pointed-with-color coats not permitted to compete in the show ring by the Cat Fanciers' Association even though they are registered by CFA. The RagaMuffin is one of the newest breeds accepted for CFA registration.

Its coat is a spectacular thick and plush display of medium-long fur. Despite its profusion, the coat is low maintenance; because it does not readily mat or clump, it requires minimum attention. The texture is dense but may vary depending on color. The hair is slightly longer around the neck and the outer edge of the face.

The RagaMuffin is a sweet-natured cat with the best traits of a devoted lap dog. It loves attention and offers the ultimate in pet companionship. It is a loving family pet offering its affection to all who want it. Although a calm cat, it is adaptive to all kind and loving family situations, even those with boisterous children, as long as it is treated with kindness and respect.

Ragdoll. According to the CFA Standard, the ideal Ragdoll is a medium-to-large, long-haired, blue-eyed, pointed cat. Ragdolls have four coat patterns: pointed, mitted, bi-color, and van.* Its point markings (paws, ears, tail tip) may be obscured by white fur covering the point color (*mitted*). Each pattern comes in six colors: seal, blue, chocolate, lilac, red, and cream. Points may be solid, lynx (tiger-striped), or tortie (tortoiseshell). The Ragdoll head is as large and broad as it is beautiful, with its well-proportioned triangle shape modified by a gently rounded muzzle. A Ragdoll's eyes are large ovals of vivid blue that stare out with serenity. Its body is long, rectangular, and broad with heavy bones. It has moderately long legs and a long plumed tail. This breed's long coat is naturally nonmatting, with a minimal woolly undercoat, which flows with the lines of the body.

A California breeder, Ann Baker, created and developed the Ragdoll in 1963. She achieved her results by crossing a combination of sturdy domestic longhairs of unknown parentage with Siamese. The foundation cat was a white domestic longhair with a sweet and gentle temperament. The cat carried Siamese-type markings known as the Himalayan

---

*Coat pattern that is all white with small colored markings on the head and tail.

pattern. Her white fur masked either a seal mitted or a black tuxedo pattern. All Ragdolls are descendants of this cat and various domestic longhair males, or from her son.

Ragdolls are well named. They are easygoing and casual and seem to lie about as if they had no bones holding them together. They are truly reminiscent of Raggedy Ann and Andy. In contradiction to this behavior, they will run to the door to greet you and follow you around from room to room. What they love to do the most is cuddle up and sleep on top of you. They are among the most gentle giants of the Cat Fancy.

Russian Blue. In the Cat Fancy, as the world of pedigreed cats and cat shows is known, *blue* is the term used for a shimmering gray coat that is so deep and rich it casts a bluish shade. In the case of the Russian Blue, the undercoat of this warm, sumptuous-looking cat is blue with each outer hair tipped in silver. Its double coat is thick, dense, water-resistant—similar to the coat of a seal or a beaver. Its large, round eyes are emerald green and as compelling as the forests of Russia. Add to this effect the lavender pink color of the paw pads and you have a dazzlingly beautiful cat. Its body is fine-boned, long, and firmly muscled. The clean lines and graceful carriage of the breed give it a regal appearance. The one allowed color by CFA for this breed is an even bright blue throughout the coat. "Lighter shades of blue [are] preferred. Guard hairs [should be] distinctly silver-tipped giving the cat a silvery sheen or lustrous appearance. A definite contrast should be noted between ground color and tipping."

It is an arctic cat; a warm double coat is a necessity for any animal living so far north. Russian Blues originated in Archangel in northern Russia and came to the North American shores at the turn of the twentieth century, via the show cat breeders of England. This elegant breed is ideally suited to a quiet environment. It is gentle and self-composed most of the time, except when it is in one of its demanding phases. It is hardly vocal at all, affectionate with its family but hesitant with visitors. It is shy and prefers not to look directly at you but will frequently change its mind and grace you with an affectionate gaze that can easily hypnotize you. An elegant, medium-sized cat, the Russian Blue does not give its friendship casually.

Scottish Fold. The unusual name for this unusual breed is easy to explain. The *Fold* part of the name refers to its ears, the top halves of which fold forward, giving it a look that seems to say, "I dare you to mention my ears." The *Scottish* part of the name obviously comes from its country of origin. According to the CFA standard, the breed came about as a spontaneous mutation in farm cats in Scotland. Those who were intrigued with the kittens established the breed by crossing British Shorthairs and domestic cats from Scotland and England with the original cat. In America, the outcrosses (other breeds introduced for their characteristics) used were the American Shorthair and the British Shorthair. However, all Scottish Folds trace their pedigree to Susie, the first fold-ear cat discovered by the founders of the breed, William and Mary Ross of Scotland.

Besides its compelling ears, another outstanding feature is the Scottish Fold's eyes, which are owl-like dollops of syrup that scrutinize you with affection and curiosity. The eyes have a wonderfully intense look. Everything about this medium-sized cat is round—its softly rounded head; its short, muscular, and roundish body; its eyes; and even its face. The breed is allowed by CFA in a wide array of colors in the solid, shaded, tabby, parti-color, and bi-color patterns.

These are good-natured cats with a warm, friendly spirit and a live-and-let-live attitude. They hardly speak, and when they do, it is with the softest mew in the cat world. Scottish Folds are prone to remaining in one place, usually sitting in a comfortable chair, for the longest time with their front legs tucked under. They are irresistible and their families tend to dote on them, giving them anything they desire, as if they are a visiting patriarch who has decided to stay.

Selkirk Rex. What immediately draws one's attention to this medium-to-large cat is its unusual-looking coat, which is very curly. The coat may be short-haired or long-haired, but unlike those of other curly-coated breeds, the curls are unstructured and seen as loose and individual. They appear to be in clumps rather than waves and are more evident around the neck, the tail, and the belly. No matter the length, the coat is usually dense, plush, and soft to the touch. Few if any cats look like this. Some breeders refer to a Selkirk Rex as a cat in sheep's clothing; still others call them a clown in lamb's clothing. Even their whiskers are curly, short, and sparse, adding to their unusual appearance. These cats have been developed as heavy-boned with surprising weight and power. They are not at all dainty. The Selkirk Rex is the result of a spontaneous mutation from a domestic housecat found in a rescue shelter in Wyoming in 1986. A Persian breeder took the one unusual-looking kitten and began developing it into a breed that eventually became the Selkirk Rex.

Unlike other breeds, the Selkirk Rex was named after the developing breeder's stepfather, Selkirk, rather than for a section of a country of origination such as the Cornish or Devon Rex. The word *rex* has been historically used to mean a coat that was not a "standard" (straight) coat. (The term is also used for some breeds of rabbits.) The breed's coat is allowed by CFA in various colors and patterns. Although these cats are like cuddly teddy bears, they are very playful and can behave like a silly child when chasing a flashlight beam or a feathery toy. However, they love nothing more than a warm lap to lie on. They are patient, loving, and very tolerant of all sorts of affectionate behavior. Intelligence, playfulness and friendliness—these are wonderful qualities in a cat.

Siamese. Since their first public appearance in the Crystal Palace Cat Show in England in 1871, the Siamese have held a special place in the hearts and minds of cat lovers everywhere. They are considered the royalty of the feline world. Legend has it that these immigrants from Siam or Burma (now Thailand and Myanmar) were the prized possessions of ancient kings and priests, who trained them to guard palaces and temples. Siamese were once stocky and round-headed; contemporary breeders have changed their look, creating the sleek, elegant competitors now seen at contemporary cat shows. The Siamese enters the show ring with a sleek, tubular-shaped body, long legs and neck, and a head that is a tapered wedge adorned with large, pointed ears and almond-shaped eyes in a deep vivid blue. These fine-boned cats are a vision of grace and elegance as they move or even as they curl up to sleep.

Their fine-textured, glossy coats lie close to the body. Those in the Cat Fancy refer to the contrasted color pattern of the coat as *colorpoint*. The *point* areas are the facial mask, the ears, the feet, and most of the tail, which are of a rich darker color in contrast to the rest of the body. Serious Siamese people allow four colors for the Siamese—seal point, chocolate point, blue point, and lilac point—and no other.

Talk to any Siamese person, and he or she will tell you that the mind of the Siamese approaches cat genius. They are highly intelligent animals with an affectionate nature.

They have a natural inclination to fetch, bow, and learn any trick you are capable of teaching them. Their voice is clear and assertive, and they will talk to you and talk to you and talk to you. When you try to read a book, your Siamese will settle down on top of it. When you write a letter, it will curl up on the paper. A Siamese wants your attention at all times.

The influence of the Siamese in the Cat Fancy is enormous especially because of its use in the creation and maintenance of other breeds. Breeds that owe much to the Siamese for their look are the Balinese, Burmese, Colorpoint Shorthair, Havana Brown, Himalayan/Persian, Javanese, Ocicat, Oriental, and Tonkinese. There are others.

Siberian. This natural breed is Russia's native cat and is not easy to find in North America no matter how commonplace it may be in Russia. The Russians refer to them as forest cats, which is to say they first made their presence known by roaming wild in the subarctic conifer forest of Siberia, known as the taiga. In this regard they resemble the rugged Norwegian Forest Cat and the Maine Coon Cat. Although they roam about the forests of Siberia in great numbers, they are also prized house cats for many Russian families, who boast of their Siberian cats' great personalities and sense of loyalty.

The Siberian is a medium to medium-large, strong cat. Its overall impression is of strength and vigilance, but with a sweet facial expression. The breed is extremely slow to mature, taking as long as five years, making patience about kittenlike behavior in young cats a necessity. The physical impression Siberians make is one of circles rather than rectangles and triangles. The breed was first imported to these shores in 1990 and was accepted for registration in the Miscellaneous Class by CFA in February 2000. Females are considerably smaller than males. Their eye color varies from gold to green. Siberians may appear in colorpoint coats and these will have blue eyes. Their triple coats are dense, water-resistant, and medium long to long. Currently the CFA standard allows all colors and patterns.

The Siberian is a wonderful home companion that will sleep with you and sit in your lap while you watch television.

Siberians adapt well to other pets and children. Although they are without fear, they are calm, laid-back cats. They are also acrobats that play hard and perform amazing somersaults chasing after a toy or some thrown object. At times a rambunctious kitten needs help after climbing up the bricks on a fireplace or to the top of a bookshelf. They remain playful throughout their lives.

The Siberian is allegedly good news for those allergic to cats, as there are those who believe that the breed is hypoallergenic. This has not been proven scientifically, however.

Singapura. The Singapura is a small-to-medium cat with a ticked coat pattern similar to that of the Abyssinian. *Ticked* refers to bands of different color on each hair. The Singapura resembles a miniature cougar with its subtle "cheetah" lines extending down from the inner corner of the eyes and its slight barring on the inner front legs and back knees. The coat covering the torso consists of dark brown ticking on an ivory ground color, with the underside the color of unbleached muslin.

Singapura is a "people" cat that develops strong attachments to its family. Its personality includes extreme curiosity blended with a striking boldness. It will jump into just about any situation and roam about, exploring kitchen counters, closets, and every conceivable hiding place within your house. It is a very friendly cat that comes right up to any visitors and fearlessly invites them to play.

Singapura is a natural breed native to Southeast Asia and named after the great island of Singapore, at the south end of the Malay Peninsula. Taken from the streets of Singapore by several Americans and imported into the United States in 1975, this uncommon breed was accepted for CFA registration in 1982 and for championship competition in 1988.

Somali. It is not enough to say that the Somali is like an Abyssinian in every way except for its medium-length coat and luxurious, bushy tail. Its double coat and full ruff give it a unique look, enhanced by long legs and elegant movements. It has a wild, feral look about it despite its gentle desire for human companionship. The original Somalis came from mating between shorthair Abyssinians with a recessive gene for long hair carried in some Abyssinian bloodlines. The body is a long type, similar to the Abyssinian: medium in length, but able to accommodate two or three dark bands of ticking. Somalis carry the Abyssinian colors: ruddy, red, or blue (blue-gray). The plumy tail is foxlike and captures the attention of those in any room through which this creature promenades.

The Somali is a highly energetic, affectionate, and extremely playful cat with an active, assertive, spirited personality. Its sudden bursts of energy and zest for everything it does has enraptured the cat-loving public for decades. Everyone who sees it is struck with admiration and awe.

Sphynx. This cat has skin like vaporized velvet—soft, warm, and smooth to the touch. It has a pleasurable feel, like caressing the warm muzzle of an affectionate horse. The Sphynx, a supposedly hairless cat, is not actually hairless. Almost imperceptible, an ever-so-slight downy fleece barely escapes the human eye but not the touch of your hand. The breed's large, batlike ears frame wide, oval-shaped saucers for eyes; the face intrigues the feline aficionado with its friendliness and intelligent expression. Because the cat has almost no coat, its substantial body is hard to recognize for what it is: that of a medium-sized cat with sturdy bones and substantial muscle development. Ideally the body should be dense, bulky, and heavy, with surprising weight for its appearance. The Sphynx is descended from a hairless kitten, a natural mutation born in Canada in 1966. It does resemble the Devon Rex without a coat.

As a kitten, the Sphynx is fun-loving and impish with a predisposition for mischief. As an adult cat, it is assertive in its desire for attention and affection and without warning will jump into the lap of someone it is courting. It enjoys being admired and looked at and will go to great lengths for admiration, from sitting in a litter box while you are trying to clean it to parking in the middle of the bed when you are changing sheets. It will greet strangers and follow them around until its presence is acknowledged. And yes, they love to eat.

Tonkinese. Although the Tonkinese is a close cousin to the Siamese and the Burmese, it differs in the shape of its body and the patterns and colors of its coat. It also combines the best behavioral qualities of those two breeds. This cat never fails to attract attention at a cat show because of its unusual looks. Everything about it involves balance, the successful blending of characteristics drawn from its two derivative breeds. The Tonkinese body is medium in length, striking a balance between the foreign shape (Siamese type) and the cobby shape (Burmese type). Registering organizations such as CFA allow it to be seen in three coat patterns—mink, full-bodied, or pointed—and their allowed colors. It is a surprisingly heavy cat with a modified wedge-shaped head, here again representing a balance between its two derivative breeds.

The Tonkinese is a fun-loving cat that is intelligent, affectionate, and full of mischief. It is very playful—too playful for some—but adjusts well to a household with children and other pets. It is alert, highly intelligent, and a warm and loving companion.

Turkish Angora. Merely the name of this cat conjures an image of a pure white, silky aristocrat, sitting on a red cushion with gold tassels like an elegant pasha bored with its power. However, the word *angora* is simply a derivative of *Ankara,* the name of the capital of Turkey, the country most identified with the breed. Of course, breeders strive for more than a cat in a solid white coat, breeding Angoras for a wide array of colors in the solid, shaded, smoke, tabby, bi-color, and parti-color patterns.

The true Angora was near extinction in the early twentieth century because Angoras crossed with Persians were replacing it. One of the oldest longhair breeds, the Angora has been long admired in its homeland. The zoo in Ankara is credited for carefully preserving the white Angora for many decades in the last century, until the cat was brought to North America in 1962, which helped to establish the breed as we know it today.

This cat is a fastidiously clean animal and prefers an immaculate home environment. Although it is playful and sociable, it is more content in a home where it is the center of attention, not having to share the spotlight with other cats. A Turkish Angora is intelligent and affectionate and wants what all cats want: close human contact, good food, and a soft, warm place to lounge about. Its eternal qualities of elegance, gracefulness, and refinement are as present today as they were hundreds of years in the past.

Turkish Van. This is an ancient, natural breed (created by nature but refined and stabilized by cat fanciers) native to eastern Turkey, a working cat from the remote, snowy regions of Lake Van, near Mount Ararat. Its body is long, broad, muscular, and deep-chested. The Turkish Van is one of the largest breeds of domestic cat, with males typically weighing from twelve to eighteen pounds and often more. Its coat is semilong, soft, with a cashmerelike texture. Its tail, or *brush,* is foxlike and strongly ringed. Ideally, the coat color should be pure chalk white and its colored markings confined to the head and tail, with one or more random body markings in the shoulder or rump areas. Cat registering organizations such as CFA allow the Van in solid-color markings plus white, tabby and white, and parti-colors and white. Although other pedigreed and nonpedigreed cats have the van coat pattern, it originated centuries ago with the Turkish Van.

Perhaps less than graceful, this alert, playful cat is highly intelligent with unique problem-solving abilities. It is a very affectionate cat that likes to curl up next to you when you read or sleep. It does not enjoy being held or carried about. The Turkish Van is especially sensitive to your change of mood and seems to know when to offer comfort and soothing behavior. Because of its high energy level, it has a hearty appetite and is capable of consuming large quantities of food. It is a unique and completely delightful companion.

F O U R

WHAT TO BUY FOR YOUR KITTEN

When you are getting ready to bring your kitten home, you'll need to consider such matters as containers to put his food in, items for his toilet needs, grooming tools, things that are acceptable for him to chew and scratch, a carrier for transport, something to sleep on, and more. Some behavior problems never start if you get your kitten the things that he needs from the beginning.

The Litter Box and Its Contents

Litter box. Without getting into the matter of training a cat (see Chapter Nine, "Training"), it is sufficient to say that you will need what amounts to an acceptable place for your kitten to use as a toilet. There are a number of options available. The most common device is a simple plastic cat pan ranging from eighteen inches to three feet in length and at least six inches high. They come in many shapes and styles. Some have A-frame covers with a round hole for an entrance in the front. The covered pans offer the cat privacy and also prevent the cat from peeing on the wall or on the floor next to the pan. Covered pans also hide the contents in the pan, making the room a more pleasant place to be.

There are mechanical and battery-operated cat boxes that offer a variety of ways to dispose of the cat's waste or separate it from the litter material. These are expensive and may or may not be effective. Also available are many elaborate (and costly) cabinets in which the litter pan is hidden from view. They can be very attractive to look at, and in some of them, it is impossible to imagine what is lurking inside. They have side openings for the cat to enter and exit and removable tops for cleaning. If you can afford them, they serve a good purpose.

Litter. The material used in the litter pan ranges from inexpensive to very expensive. The least expensive materials are sand and strips of cut-up newspaper. These are practically cost free. However, they may not do a satisfactory job of masking the looks and the odors of urine and fecal matter and must be changed multiple times a day.

The manufacturing of litter box material has become a major industry. There are numerous types available in supermarkets and pet supply stores. You can purchase plain granulated clay, deodorizing pellets, flushable litter, wood chips, or litter with various additives from baking soda to perfume-type chemicals. This is a trial-and-error process that is best left up to your kitten. Some kittens prefer one type to the exclusion of all others. Finding the one litter that your cat prefers may help avoid future toileting "accidents." Try dif-

ferent materials and brands and watch the cat use them. Many cats, for example, refuse to use scented litters, while others will not accept a change once you've started with one or the other. In the matter of flushable cat litter, check with your plumber first.

Rake. You will need a special tool to rake through the litter pan every day or as often as necessary to keep it clean and free of fecal matter. The rake is an aluminum or plastic slotted, modified spoon, about ten inches long. It will remove solid material from the pan without taking the gravel or litter out. It is a necessary utensil for keeping the litter pan clean.

Plastic liners. These have become very popular and for good reason. Plastic liners are manufactured to fit the various sizes of litter pans. They line the inner surfaces and make it easy to remove the used cat litter by gathering the edges of the liner up at the top and pulling it out like a sack. With the litter entirely removed, it is less tedious to wash out the pan. The only glitch may be if your kitten doesn't like the feel of the plastic liner beneath his paws. It is worth a try, though, because of the work saved.

Bowls and What to Put in Them

Bowls. The type of food and water container you prefer is a matter of personal taste, so to speak. Many experienced cat owners and breeders prefer medium to small stainless steel bowls with shallow sides. There are those designed for small dogs and those designed for cats; there is not much difference between the two. Steel bowls are easier to keep clean than plastic bowls and last for the life of your cat. You can use the same kind of bowl for solid food as for water, but you will need one for each. However, a small, flat dish for canned or cooked food is what a cat likes best. When you first offer food to your kitten, he is going to be cautious and somewhat doubtful about it. A dish will make it easier for him to examine and smell the food before eating it. A small plate also makes it easer for a kitten to get to the food; it al-

lows him to do what he likes best with food—separate one morsel from the others.

It is a good idea to place the food and water containers on a nonporous place mat to catch the spilt crumbs and water.

Small plastic and ceramic bowls designed for cats are also serviceable. However, some ceramic bowls, though pleasantly decorated, are not fired at high-enough temperatures in the manufacturer's kiln, thus allowing the lead content of the glaze to leach through and possibly cause lead poisoning.

Self-feeding containers, some of which will hold an enormous amount of dry cat food and some of which are meant to hold large amounts of water, can be quite convenient. They are tall, vertical containers with a small dishlike cup at the bottom. As the cat nibbles away, emptying the cup, gravity encourages the dry food to refill it.

There are also mechanical and battery-operated feeding dishes that resemble a flat-lying clock and turn to an opening on a timed basis, revealing a measured portion of dry food. These are meant for those who cannot remember to feed their cat or need to leave them alone for more than a day.

Cat food. Be prepared to feed your kitten soon after his arrival. The best idea is to obtain a one-week supply of the food that he has been getting. *Do not change your cat's diet suddenly.* A sudden change may cause diarrhea or vomiting at a time when your kitten needs maximum nutrition for growth. Introduce any new food gradually, along with the regular diet. For two days use 25 percent of the new diet with 75 percent of the old diet. Mix it thoroughly. For two more days use 50 percent of the new diet with 50 percent of the old diet and mix it. For the next two days use 75 percent of the new diet with 25 percent of the old diet. Mix it together. On the seventh day feed the new diet exclusively. This is the surest way to avoid upsetting your cat's stomach with a new cat food.

Consult your cat breeder or a veterinarian for a type and amount of food to give to your new kitten. Feed him in a calm, relaxed atmosphere. For more feeding information, refer to Chapter Eight, "Feeding the Kitty."

The Cat Bed

When you provide a bed for your new kitten, you will be doing more than providing a place to sleep; you will be appealing to his sense of territory, thus satisfying a basic cat need. All cats, young and old alike, seek out a soft, cozy place to sleep. Over the years he will try napping on every conceivable place in your home, from your own bed to the sofa to your underwear drawer. However, he may return to the one place that is personally scented and securely located. A small wicker or plastic basketlike bed with a soft pillow or

Tall. carpet-covered poles with enclosed platforms at the top are brilliantly conceived for the cat who can have everything.

blanket is all that he needs. Most cats appreciate one that is covered so that it is somewhat like a small cave. Tall, carpet-covered poles with enclosed platforms at the top are brilliantly conceived. Carpeted cat furniture is highly desirable although somewhat costly. It also takes up space in a small apartment.

It really doesn't matter to the cat whether you spend hundreds of dollars or simply line a cardboard carton with something soft. A kitten appreciates a space of his own, some place to hang his tail and call home. Try to locate the cat bed in a snug corner on a higher level than the floor. Cats like high places. You are sure to find your kitten or grown cat some day on your highest book shelf, sleeping or watching over his realm.

Something to Scratch

This is an important subject for you as well as your kitten because some forethought here will help you avoid potentially destructive behavior. You must carefully consider your kitten's need to scratch certain surfaces with his nails. This is what cat scratching is all about. It is essential to understand that cats scratch with their claws because of a physical and psychological need to do so. Cats develop behavior patterns early in their lives that are difficult to change; unless you set the proper behavior patterns early, your kitten is going to scratch whatever is handy and appealing, and it will be extremely difficult to break the habit once he is old enough to be destructive. Refer to Chapter Ten, "The Short and Sweet Problem Solver." You must have a *scratch post* of some kind

in your home, preferably before your kitten arrives. Many cats and their owners have parted company on the issue of destroying furniture and other possessions through this necessary behavior. An untrained cat with an urge to dig his nails into something is capable of destroying thousands of dollars worth of furniture, carpeting, curtains, and bedding, not to mention expensive clothing that is lying around.

You must provide your kitten with something to scratch his nails on that is satisfying for him and acceptable to you. The most typical scratching implement is the vertical scratch post, which is usually a wooden post attached to a flat base and covered with carpet, canvas, or burlap. Cats will use it instead of your furniture *if it is tall enough*. A grown cat must have something so high that he can scratch reaching up with his front nails when standing on his hind legs. There is nothing more useless than a scratch post that is too short. However, an effective scratch post can also be a long log lying horizontally or leaning vertically against the wall if it is secured to the floor. There are many versions of scratch posts, some of which are made of cork or nubby fabric. Cats do not like to scratch tightly woven fabric; burlap and nubby materials are best for scratching.

Then there is the wide variety of *cat furniture*, which is meant to be both scratched and used as a lair for napping. Cat furniture of all sizes, shapes, and types provide excellent coverings that cats enjoy clawing. The more expensive pieces are tall, elaborate treelike structures with several carpeted platforms and covered enclosures that form a feline playground. Although they are costly and take up a good bit of room, they are an excellent source of pleasure and security for your cat. Most cats and kittens take to them immediately. You can find them advertised in cat magazines, in pet supply stores, and in mail-order catalogs. They are always on display by vendors at cat shows.

A highly effective option to avoid the scratching problem is the use of a disposable scratch pad, which is inexpensive and readily available. A pad is made of a rectangular piece of corrugated cardboard approximately 24 inches long and 6 inches wide. It is rubbed with a small amount of catnip to encourage the cat to use it. Place your kitten on it as a resting place and gently rub his front paws against the rough surface. Chances are his nails will unsheathe and dig into the surface. It will be pleasant for him, and he will learn to use it whenever he likes. Once a kitten begins to use a disposable scratch pad, he will tend not to scratch anyplace else. By the way, you can turn the corrugated insert over when the initial surface is scratched smooth. Many cats enjoy these scratch pads and use them as a place to sleep.

Leash, Harness, Collar, and ID Tag

Leash. A leash is completely unnecessary if you have no plans for walking with your kitten outdoors. However, a leash can be useful for other purposes having to do with safety and restraint. For example, you may want your cat on a leash when holding him as you get into a car or to keep him available for nail clipping, bathing, or visits to the veterinarian where there is a possibility of losing control.

Leashes designed specifically for cats are made of nylon, lightweight and comfortable. The leash must be strong enough to prevent the cat from getting away from you yet light enough so that it is not an irritating burden. Nylon cat leashes are colorful, lightweight, and almost stringlike in appearance. *Never use a dog leash, string, twine, rope, or yarn.*

Harness. The proper equipment to accompany a leash is a cat harness. Like a cat leash, these are made of lightweight nylon, and they are most often purchased as a set with a nylon leash. Harnesses are available in figure-eight format, figure-H format, or other formats. They are mostly made of a stretchable material.

Collar. There is only one good reason for using a collar on a cat and that is to attach an ID tag or license to it. It should not be used with a leash. If you plan to show your cat, it is best not to use a collar at all, as the collar may damage the coat around the neck. Although a kitten should be introduced to the idea of a collar early, it is best to start out with something innocuous, such as a light piece of ribbon tied loosely around the neck. Allow the cat to wear this continually. If the ribbon does not distract your pet, you may replace it with the actual collar in a day or two. It is very important for a cat collar to be very elastic and stretchy or even breakable by the cat so that it cannot strangle him if it gets snagged on anything. Some collars have a short length of elastic sewn onto the leather, while others are made with Velcro tape so that they will actually pull apart with pressure.

ID tag. All cats should wear an ID tag (except when in the show ring), whether they are allowed to go outdoors or not. Proper identification can prevent permanent loss if the cat accidentally gets out and becomes lost. Have an ID tag made up at your local pet supply store. Have the cat's name and your last name engraved on the metal along with your phone number. Engraved information does not usually rub off and disappear.

Other forms of identification. There is now available an identification microchip about the size of a grain of rice that can be surgically implanted beneath the surface of the cat's skin. It contains information about your cat that can be registered with the manufacturer. It can be read with a hand-held scanner. Ask a veterinarian, staff at an animal shelter, or a registering organization such as the Cat Fanciers' Association about this procedure.

Among the most important tools for retrieving a lost or stolen cat is a complete set of photos showing a front and side view of the cat along with a close-up of the face. One dated photo of you holding the cat is a convincing argument for settling questions of ownership.

Cat Carrier

You will need a special container capable of safely transporting your cat from one place to another. Although you may think an ordinary box will do, you are going to change your mind after your first experience with your cat outside your home. You must have a sturdy, reliable travel case. The best cat carrier is the hard, rigid type, made of thick, strong plastic—a small traveling cage versatile enough for local use or for the rigors of long-distance auto or air travel. The small cage-type carrier has a door in the front made of thin metal bars and must be *well* ventilated with small holes on the top and sides. The door is secured with a spring-loaded latch easily squeezed open with your fingers but impossible for a cat to disengage. The luggage-type handle makes it easy to

carry. An important aspect of this type of carrier is that it meets airline requirements even though you may only use it to take your kitten to the vet's office.

Carrying cases come in a number of styles, types, and prices. An older style but very much in use is the solid, suitcase type carrier, which opens at the top. The top is made of transparent plastic so the cat can see what's going on. You hold it with a hard luggage handle attached to the top. It must have ventilation holes on all sides.

Also available are soft, fabric-type carriers, much like modern luggage that is lightweight and easy to tote by hand or over the shoulder. Small patches of mesh screening on the sides allow for good ventilation. Although highly attractive and convenient for short trips to the vet's office, they are impractical and unsafe for auto or air travel.

Grooming Tools

Nail trimmers. You should start grooming your kitten at a young age so that he makes a quick adjustment to the various procedures. The most important grooming you must start with is nail trimming. Nail trimmers for cats are specially designed; nothing else should be used. Trimmers come in three types. There is the *scissor* type, which is small with blunt ends instead of points. The blades form a circular hole in which you place the nail and then snip. There is also the *safety nail trimmer,* which resembles a pair of pliers with a spring between the handles. It too functions as a scissors with a circular hole in the blades, but it has a safety stop to limit the length of the nail that is cut. In addition, there is the *guillotine trimmer,* a cross between a pair of pliers and a cigar cutter. The nail is placed in the hole at the end of the tool and the handles are squeezed together, causing a sharp blade to slide across, slicing off the exposed bit of nail.

Comb and brush. Short-coated kittens require a bristle or rubber-type brush only. As the kitten matures, a comb will be a useful addition. Long- or medium-coated kittens need a stainless steel comb with blunt, round-edge teeth, designed for cats, plus a natural-bristle brush. Although combing and brushing are not all that necessary for most kittens, it is advisable to start grooming as early as possible if only to get the cat used to it.

Cat Toys

Play is an activity that is as significant for kittens as it is for children. Yes, it is a source of pleasure and diversion and exercise, but it is much more meaningful than that. If you have ever had the privilege of watching a litter of kittens at play,

you may have noticed that it all boils down to an innocent-looking form of fighting and wrestling. However, play is in reality a learning and practicing process for stalking, ambushing, and attacking prey animals. Play is essentially a dress rehearsal for adult life.

Play is greatly enhanced by cat toys. If you attend cat shows, you will find vendors selling many toys designed for interaction between you and your cat and for independent play. Among these are peacock feathers and various small fishing poles with string and shiny slivers dangling from them. Waving these toys in front of your kitten's eyes in a bouncing motion, tickling the nose and feet, all stimulate the hunter in your pet and will divert him for quite a while. Of course, you can use a string or a short length of rope in the same way.

A hard rubber ball, a table tennis ball, an empty spool of thread are excellent cat toys along with all the manufactured mice rubbed with catnip. Toys involving table tennis balls that circle around in a track can occupy a cat for hours. Among the very best cat toys is a simple sheet of paper crumpled up and tossed across the room or a beam from a flashlight teasingly moved across the floor. The play's the thing.

Becoming friends is the first and most necessary step
toward successfully living with a cat.

FIVE

MAKING FRIENDS WITH YOUR NEW KITTEN

Without getting too sloppy about it, your goal with a new kitten from the first moment you meet should be to create a close, emotional tie with the youngster. Cat experts call it *bonding*, but it is essentially making friends. Some animals living in the wild form a *pair-bond*, which in animal terms is a relationship between two creatures that develop an attachment and dependency on each other. Through the course of their lives, they live together, travel together, and try never to lose each other.

Bonding also occurs between people, whether they are husband and wife, parent and child, friends or lovers. It is the ideal relationship between humans and their kittens. To bond with your pet you must first understand that kittens are highly complicated organisms with a genetically organized set of natural behaviors. In other words, a cat's gotta do what a cat's gotta do.

Despite the tender emotions of parenthood, you must set aside the idea of your new kitten as a novelty and relate to him as a living, breathing youngster that needs love, sustenance, and firm guidance. Your kitten will soon learn, if you do the right things, that you are his protector and provider as well as the source of love, affection, and friendship. You are all that stands between this helpless, vulnerable babe and the dangers beyond your front door. You are the teacher, the judge, and the giver of physical and emotional nourishment. Make no mistake, it is a large responsibility but one that most adults (and even many children) are capable of handling. Some day soon, when your kitten has grown to adulthood, he will find a way to say thanks for your being there.

Bonding, the Essence of Friendship

As Humphrey Bogart says to Claude Rains in the final scene of *Casablanca*, "Louie, I think this is the beginning of a beautiful friendship." So is your new life with a kitten.

Bonding with your kitten means creating a personal relationship between the two of you based on genuine feelings of affection. Cats that have bonded with their families usually have a strong desire to be with them. They have developed a sense of belonging to their home, which to a cat means his territory. Making friends with your kitten not only satisfies his instinctive needs, it also gets him to accept you as teacher and trainer and promotes good behavior. Bonding definitely makes life more pleasant for everyone.

No matter what your kitten's previous life was like, you have an opportunity to communicate to him that he is safe, cherished, and respected. (This is also true for a cat that has already been living with you for a while. It is never too late to change the relationship with him for the better, even if he is older.) Bonding involves communicating your affection, introducing him to his new home, feeding him, speaking to him, touching him, using body language, playing with him, and responding to all manner of kitten activities.

On Arrival

The arrival of a kitten in any household causes quite a stir. Children are the most excitable, but never underestimate the emotional outburst of many adults too. Get the introductions over with as quickly and as quietly as possible. Try to avoid loud noises, bright lights, too much handling and fondling of the new arrival along with overwhelming attention and expressions of affection. These may frighten your kitten, which will make him anxious about his new surroundings. He has no idea where he is or who these creatures are and whether they are going to harm him or not. It is your job to convince this newcomer that he is in good hands.

The very first thing to do is to allow the kitten to take a look and a sniff at the new home. Do not give him the complete run of the house, though. Take him into one room at a time, allowing him to see the entire territory and range. Do not allow the newcomer to roam from you or it may take hours to find him. Show him his litter pan right away and teach him how to use it (see Chapter Nine, "Training").

Holding Your Kitten

Holding a cat properly is more important than you would imagine. Avoid holding a cat in any way that scares him. He may panic and try to squirm away, and in the process you may be scratched or the cat may have a bad fall. You can easily avoid this danger when you know how to pick him up.

With the kitten facing away from you, simply slide your hand along his belly and up to his chest; stop when your fingers are just behind the front legs. Place the cat's rear end and back legs in the open palm of your other hand. Be firm but gentle and it will be almost impossible to lose your grip or allow the youngster to get away from you. It will appear that you are presenting the kitten to the rest of the world. If you reverse this and allow him to face you, he is going to dig his nails into your shirt and that will hurt and you may drop him. This is how to lift a kitten as well as an adult cat. It is the first step toward making your kitten feel secure.

Communicating Your Affection

Now that you know how to hold your kitten, you should begin to communicate your affection toward him. You may lift him up, hold him as described above, and add a gentle hug, a kiss on the top of his head, and a playful squeeze of

You cannot be too affectionate with a kitten at this point unless you physically smother him.

the paws. You cannot be too affectionate with a kitten at this point unless you physically smother him. Do not hold back.

Naming

It is essential to select your kitten's name right away and begin using it immediately. Naming a cat is a subjective matter; it doesn't matter how elaborate or simple or literary the name you choose, as long as it is dignified and loving. It is best to have a one-syllable call name in addition, because that is the one you will probably use most of the time anyway. Pets learn one-syllable names quickly and respond best to them, especially if they associate something pleasant with the sound of the name. At first, kneel down, hold out a food tidbit or commercial treat and call the kitten to you by his name. He will probably come right away if the tidbit has an odor he likes. As he sniffs it, say his name and then something very affectionate. If you do this often enough he will not only learn his name quickly, he will always associate it with something rewarding, even if it is just a scratch behind the ear and a sweet greeting. This is also a way of teaching him to come to you when you call him.

Talking

The sound of your voice and its intonation are two key elements in the bonding process. Have you ever watched the parents and friends of a young baby? Listen to the ridiculous things they say and the way they say them. Then watch the baby's face. The baby may smile, even giggle, or become quiet as he takes in the sounds with wide-eyed fascination. Everything is input to a new baby, and everything you do or say has an effect.

The same is true for your new kitten. When you speak to him, he listens and then responds. The softer your voice, the sweeter and the higher-pitched it is, the more concentrated

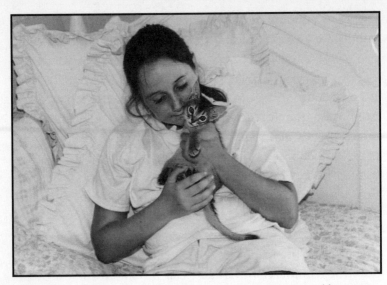

Touching creates warmth and intimacy between cats and humans.

will his response be to it. A cat's hearing is much more acute than human hearing. If you raise your voice in anger, your kitten will react with fear because he is highly sensitive to loud sounds. Anger is also easily understood by anyone and to a cat is quite frightening. If you use a moderate, loving tone of voice, your kitten will want to be near you. The affectionate use of your voice is one of the most important tools you have to help you bond with your kitten as well as influence good behavior. It will serve both of you for the rest of your lives together.

Being Aware of Body Language

Most people living with small animals rarely consider the effect of their body language on the family pet. Your body does communicate messages to your kitten or adult cat that can be more powerful than what you say. Body language is not complicated at all. The underlying rule is to be as nonthreatening in manner or gesture as possible. Bear in mind that a cat, especially a kitten, is by comparison to a human a very small creature. Therefore, do not stand so close that you tower over him, forcing him to move out of your way. Inexperienced kittens may follow you around so closely that they intertwine between your feet and get stepped on. It is always best when possible to kneel down to the cat's level so that he can relate to you without feeling threatened. Do not make sharp, unfriendly moves when you are close to the cat. Sudden or jerky gestures also have a negative effect on a kitten. Strive for an easy, soft manner with your kitten.

Introductions

The kitten's introduction to his new home is critical. Everyone in the family should have a turn greeting him, and by all means expressing their affection by holding him properly and talking to him sweetly, but do it one person at a time. Keep the kitten away from any other pets in the home until they can meet in a quiet and highly supervised atmosphere. Otherwise the kitten will find a hiding place and stay there for hours, cowering in fear. This not only delays the bonding process but can set it back.

Feeding

Nothing creates a bond quicker and more strongly than feeding your kitten. Whoever feeds the cat becomes his nurturing caretaker, a significant role in a cat's life. The one who feeds him in a sense becomes a substitute mother. The first few feedings offer an important opportunity for bonding. To put it simply, feed your cat with affection. Make a fuss about it with a stream of happy, upbeat talk as you go to the cupboard and pull down the food, open it, pour it into the bowl, and place it at the designated feeding place. After a few feedings, your kitten will quickly learn all your gestures leading up to renewed food in the bowl. He will start responding to

The one who feeds him in a sense becomes a substitute mother.

this routine and follow your movements. As you get out the food and place it in the bowl, do not bring it directly to the cat. Let the cat come to it. This is the time to establish desirable habits, so show him where to eat and drink by placing the bowl in the chosen location. As you place the bowl down, pet the kitty on the top of his head and then let him eat in peace. Fresh water should be present, in another bowl, of course.

Playing

Playing with your cat is an important part of friendship. The correct way to play with your cat is in a positive, nonthreatening manner. Get down on the floor and make yourself available to climb on or rub against. Avoid play that encourages aggressive behavior. Do not indulge in tug-of-war and pulling legs or tails. You do not want to create a relationship based on bitten fingers or a scratched face. If the kitten misbehaves, do not holler or hit or punish him in any way. You wouldn't do that to a baby, and you shouldn't do it to a kitten.

Making friends with your kitten helps introduce him to his environment and teaches him the routines of his new life. Maintain an attitude of teaching without punishments or harsh corrections. Play with your cat often, at different times of the day and evening. Give him several periods of exercise involving tossed toys and rolled balls and ending with small food treats. Develop in the kitten's mind his feeding place, his sleeping place, and where he may and may not go. Introducing your kitten to his new life and the gentle, loving way you do it are all part of the process of bonding.

SIX

BASIC CAT BEHAVIOR:
WHY THEY DO WHAT THEY DO

If you can crack the code of the feline mystique, you will enter the world of the perfect purr. It is an adventure. The feline mystique is no more or less than the basic behavior of cats, which is the foundation on which a cat's day-to-day behavior rests. If you want to enjoy the feline experience with peace of mind and the ability to cope with the sometimes baffling or up-setting behavior of your kitten, then you must have some grasp of what to expect in terms of their natural, basic behavior.

The greatest mistake a kitten owner can make is to think of the newcomer as a human and not as a cat. This is not to say that there aren't similarities between relating to a human child and relating to a kitten. Long-enduring relationships between humans and domestic cats develop along lines similar to those between parent and child. The instant a human assumes the responsibility of protecting, feeding, and caring for a cat, he or she is creating a form of juvenile dependency in the animal. This juvenile behavior may always remain as part of the cat's personality, but so do various aspects of its natural or basic behavior, which simply lie in a dormant state ready for the right situation to trigger them. If you doubt this, wait until your pampered puss encounters its first mouse or injured bird and see what happens. Don't be shocked. It is the same sweet kitty cat sleeping on your lap that can dispatch a prey animal to a violent destiny.

One can see in the domestic cat a paradox of behavior. The skill of the solitary hunter produces an adult capable of instant self-sufficiency. The acceptance of loving care produces a variation of eternal kittenhood. Therefore, our beloved house cats are both independent and dependent at the same time. This may be the only difference between wild and domestic cats other than size and lifestyle. It is also an important part of your kitten's mystery.

Of course, you can expect specific behavioral differences from breed to breed. For example, most Persians, Ragdolls, Birmans, and Scottish Folds are easygoing and would rather sit around and watch you than follow you around like a Siamese, Abyssinian, or Devon Rex. Any cat expert will tell you that cats are all highly individual creatures with many exceptions to the rule. However, all of the aspects of basic feline behavior covered here are based on what is known about cats in a general way, as they would have lived out their lives in a natural or wild state. All cats play out these behaviors, whether or not they make sense in your home.

Territory

The term *territory* simply refers to an area an animal regularly inhabits and in which it carries out most of its activities for survival. A cat takes territory very seriously and behaves as though this area is an extension of itself; it may accept some intruders or it may attempt to drive them away. A cat in the wild may inherit its territory, win it in combat, or discover it and claim it after its abandonment by a previous feline. Of course, pet cats are simply plopped into our homes and that's that. Nevertheless, that kitten grows up in its home with as powerful a sense of territory as if it were living in a jungle.

Territory is not always a fixed bit of real estate. For cats, territories can be loosely fixed areas influenced by time, space, and other creatures. This flexibility is what allows domestic cats, which are essentially solitary creatures, to adapt to multicat situations.

Territory is claimed and defended (often aggressively) as an instinctive drive for the purpose of survival. It is an intense drive. When its people move to another house, the family cat may become depressed and very upset and may attempt to escape in order to return to the former residence because that is the cat's territory; eventually it adjusts to the new home. Most mammals inherently struggle for territory in order to protect their food supply and procreate in safety. Despite the many generations of domesticity in the typical house cat, the instinct to claim and defend territory is quite strong.

There are two important locations that define a cat's territory. The first is the *core area* or *immediate home*, which receives the heaviest use. The immediate home area is where most daily activities take place. It also contains the lair, the safest sleeping area in the entire territory. In domesticity, the core area may be an entire house, one room in an apartment, a portion of a room, or even your bed. The second area is the *home* or *outer range*. In the wild this is a vague, loosely defined area composed of interconnecting pathways and trails leading to water, resting places, scent posts, emergency retreats, and favorite sunning spots. It is also where most hunting takes place. The home range may be an entire valley or portion of a mountain range for some of the larger wild cats. For domestic cats, it may be a basement, a kitchen, garage, back alley, or yard.

Male cats claim larger territories than females. Female cats are especially intolerant of territorial intrusions from other female cats. Quite frequently the outer ranges of neighboring cats overlap, a situation that is tolerated because the territoriality of cats also has to do with time. Neighboring cats may hunt the same terrain but at different times. They will try to avoid each other at all costs. This scheduled use of space prevents confrontations and fighting, except about sex. It is quite a different situation from the sharing of common territory by two or more cats that live with a human family. Here an informal order of rank and superiority coupled with the cats' juvenile tendencies helps maintain order and a peaceful atmosphere.

Animal behavior regarding territory varies by species from casual to intense. All cats, wild and domestic, have strong responses concerning the acquisition and defense of territory. Domestic cats rarely have the opportunity to choose their territory. Even so, once they are brought to a place, they relate to it as their wild cousins do. Animals who graze in a herd, such as wildebeests, and those who hunt in a pack, such as wolves, travel vast distances in a sprawling, ill-defined territory, creating a great overlap of ranges. Consequently, their attitude toward territory is much more casual than that of cats.

With the exception of lions, cats in the wild live and hunt for the most part alone. Their hunting techniques involve stalking and ambushing, lunging and pouncing. Their territories are smaller and more exclusive than those of other mammals. Few cats in the wild can afford to tolerate an incursion into their territory by other cats. This fact is of vital importance to cat owners because it explains why their pets may become upset with a new cat, a human they do not trust, visiting cats, or a move to a new house. From the family cat's point of view, any change affecting territory is a threat to its survival.

These tendencies are made apparent by the degree of emotion shown when the cat's territory is violated or moved. The most common expression of emotional distress is for a cat to urinate and defecate in various parts of the new premises (territory) instead of in its litter box. Sometimes the cat behaves as though it is depressed, and it may well be. An unhappy cat may make low, throaty sounds you never heard before and may even start clawing the furniture, the walls, the curtains, or the nearest person. Claiming territory in the wild also involves scratching the ground and specific trees. Although relationships with humans and other animals become very important to domestic cats, loss of territory is of even greater importance. It is taken as a catastrophe. While a domestic cat assumes it will survive without you, instinct tells the cat that it is in jeopardy with the loss of established territory. This grievous fear is usually not based in fact, because the human has simply exchanged one territory for another. But the cat doesn't know this; you will need great patience and much extra soothing and attention to convince the cat that he is still safe when he is uprooted from his territory and moved somewhere else.

An extremely important aspect of territory for the cat owner to understand has to do with *marking*. *Marking* means the acts by which a cat in the wild or at home leaves his individual sign of identity in various parts of the immediate home or the home range, or on another cat's territory. Researchers are not entirely sure of the reasons for territory marking and can only offer educated guesses.

Some believe it is used as a boundary demarcation so that

wandering or visiting cats will know they are trespassing. However, few cats have ever been reported to turn in the opposite direction on coming upon a territory mark. It may be a guide for cats to avoid each other and thus prevent sudden clashes. A major purpose of territory marking is to send a message about mating. Marking, frequently accomplished with pungent urine, becomes a perfumed love letter, so to speak.

Cats mark their territory in several ways. The most common and least understood by new cat owners has to do with the cat's toileting habits. All cats, male and female, *spray* as a means of marking territory. When a cat marks territory or asserts itself, which are closely related motives, he will back up against a vertical object, such as a wall or a tree, and spray it with highly scented urine. He may also defecate (and bury it), scratch or claw an object, wipe his paws on it, or vocalize like a little lion. Quite often, cats employ more than one of these methods at the same time. This information can be of some help to the cat owner who doesn't understand why the family cat has suddenly "gone crazy" with unacceptable behavior.

Many cat owners assume that the spraying of sexually scented urine by male cats will stop once the animal has been castrated. This expectation is one of the primary reasons pet owners have this surgical procedure done. (There are other important reasons for neutering a male cat, not the least of which is preventing him from mating and helping to produce unwanted litters of kittens.) But experienced cat owners will tell you that altering a male does not always prevent spraying. Once this behavior has set in, spraying must be approached as a training problem as well as a physical problem.

When spraying, male cats (as well as some females) will back up against a wall, a window, a piece of furniture, or some outdoor object and spray urine. In the case of unaltered male cats, this urine usually smells unpleasant. Every breed and nonbreed of cat, every variety of cat behaves in this manner. It is the most common form of marking.

Spraying, although usually a form of sexual communication by either male or female, can also be used by a cat as a sign of defiance to another cat after a nonviolent confrontation. This marking will occur at various spots already sprayed in the past as territory marks. In your cat's litter box, the feces are usually buried beneath the sand. But on occasion the cat will bury the old feces and display the new feces on top of the mound. This act may be accompanied by a throaty sound and a mad dash from room to room. Sometimes the cat runs in a stiff, sideways gait that is not unlike its arched display when preparing for a confrontation. Sometimes the cat's performance appears as if it were triumphant.

Marking territory or communicating the cat's presence is all too often accomplished by clawing visible scratches into a vertical object such as a tree, if you're lucky, or the arm of a sofa, if you're not. Although most scratching has to do with the need to remove the outer sheath of the claws, some of it has to do with assertion and the marking of territory.

The Instinct to Hunt

Cats living without the benefits of a human family do not get pull-tab cans of gourmet cat food in delectable gravies, no plastic-lined bags of fresh granular miracles expertly formulated with nutritional genius, wafting heavenly odors for the feline palate. In a wild setting dinner runs, crawls, or flies and it requires four swift legs to be caught. A hungry cat must be clever, patient, and fast when opportunity presents itself. All of its natural instincts must come into play. Even though cats are among the keenest hunters in the animal kingdom, in nature's restaurant, dinner does not always end with an entrée.

No one knows for sure if cats stalk, kill, and eat prey animals because they are hungry or because their hunting instincts are triggered when they see natural prey run or fly from them. As some adventurers climb mountains because they are there, cats apparently chase mice for the same reason, as well as birds, butterflies, and even houseflies. If you have ever lived with a cat, you know that they all become intensely curious about scratching sounds, high-pitched squealing noises, sudden motions, and things that flutter and try to fly away. Most cat toys cater to these instincts. These stimulations are associated not necessarily with any specific prey animal but simply with the desire for catching prey. The cat quickly moves to the source of the sound and investigates visually and possibly by sniffing. All the hunting mechanisms shift into gear at the first sighting of movement, or sooner, if the cat is an adult, experienced hunter. The first sign of hunting behavior is a stalking motion.

A young, inexperienced cat tends to regard all small creatures as harmless objects of curiosity or even as fellow cats. A cat and a mouse placed together do not necessarily play out the drama of the hunter and the hunted. The cat's prey-catching instincts dictate that if the mouse moves slowly, it will be sniffed but tolerated. However, if the mouse runs away from the cat swiftly, in a straight line, the cat will chase it and pounce on it. This is true when very small animals run away from or at right angles to a cat. When a smaller animal runs *to* the cat, the cat will hesitate and perhaps retreat. Specific directions of movement automatically release his catching action. It all seems to be part of the feline genetic code. Only prey with fur or a furlike covering will elicit a bite that kills. The prey's scent seems to have little or no bearing on stalking or killing. A cat primarily uses scent for the purpose of mating and investigating food, although the hunting instincts can come into play through scent if dried urine spots are left by fleeing mice. Cats on the hunt will sniff along this type of trail to find the mouse's entry and exit into open range.

Cats have a remarkable memory for the places where they have traveled. A cat that experiences a hunting triumph at a particular location will remember that exact place and return again and again seeking another triumph, even after a long time has elapsed. This memory is an extremely important part of the cat's superb hunting ability and has obvious survival value. Understanding it is helpful when you have your first kitten.

Humans often misconstrue as "cruel" what domestic cats usually do with their captured prey, and certainly it is behavior that is difficult to reconcile with the cuddly and lovable image of the pet kitten. Adult cats appear to play with their captured prey until it mercifully dies or they kill it. This instinctive behavior is part of the cat's genetic composition to teach kittens how to chase and capture a living meal. Its purpose is to elicit the correct response in kittens so that their hunting instincts may develop properly.

Both novice and experienced cat owners must understand that their pets are *natural* creatures with a strong set of behaviors designed for survival. Nature never anticipated the concept of domestic pets living in safety and comfort. Most living organisms have, built into their behavior, the drive to ensure the survival of their species. This is why most animals protect and teach their young what they need to know. Bear this in mind if you witness your cat's behavior with captured prey. It is best not to interfere. Consider what the captured animal probably does with *its* prey. Beyond rainbows, golden sunsets, and grazing deer, the unembellished truth is that nature can be harsh and often violent. The good news is that human sensitivities have interceded and softened some of these behaviors.

What constitutes the prey of domestic cats? A cat will be attracted to any living animal no bigger than itself. Depending on the cat's aggressive inclinations, he is mostly interested in mice. Domestic cats are also interested in most insects, including moths, butterflies, houseflies, beetles, crickets, and grasshoppers. They are also interested in frogs, toads, lizards, snakes, rabbits, shrews, moles, squirrels, birds, and even an occasional praying mantis.

With regard to birds, bird and cat lovers can be reassured that cats are capable of catching only old, sick, wounded, or very young birds. Only on rare occasions do cats capture mature, healthy birds. At least three-fourths of all birds die as a result of nature's own control of the population-to-territory ratio. The primary factors that reduce the bird population are cold weather, insufficient food, and disease. Cats could never survive on a diet of birds exclusively. In fact, cats perform an important function when they prey on unprotected, old, sick, or injured birds. By selecting out these from the rest of the flock, they enhance the survival of the general bird population.

The method of catching prey is what makes the cat, domestic and wild, the consummate hunter of the entire animal kingdom. A cat usually hears its prey first. Only on rare occasions does it sight its quarry first. In a crouched posture, the cat will run toward the sound. He then stops and observes in a close-to-the-ground position. In a natural setting he would crouch behind grass, earth mounds, or other forms of cover. The principal technique is to ambush the prey animal before it has the opportunity to escape. In a stooped-shoulder manner, he waits for the prey to move or show itself. Domestic cats are quite patient and capable of waiting long periods of time. Once the prey is sighted, the cat employs a stalking run, which again is very low to the ground. This enables him to get closer to the prey without giving away his presence or having to give chase. More observation takes place as the claws unsheathe; the tail lies flat and twitches from side to side at the tip, and the leg muscles contract in readiness to spring. Every sense the cat possesses goes into full operation, from extended whiskers to forward-pointing ears. With a wobbling motion of the hind legs, the cat prepares to attack. He springs forward, low to the ground, and races to the victim and pounces in a shallow leap. The cat almost always catches the mouse with his paws at this stage. To watch it do so is to see nature in all its graceful brutality.

Experienced cat owners know that not every cat will chase, catch, kill, or eat mice. A domestic cat may perform none or one or any combination of these predatory elements. Although there is no way to be sure why this is true, there are some possible explanations for this behavior (or lack of it). Every cat has the inherent tendency to hunt for food. Whether or not this instinct is developed fully depends on several factors. It must be elicited at an early age by the mother, by the littermates, and by the prey itself. However, even if there is no early elicitation of the prey-catching behaviors, they will appear later with the onset of hunger or with the appearance of prey animals acting in a manner that provokes this behavior.

Researchers have observed that a kitten makes the first

prey-catching movement at about three weeks of age. This is a tentative forward grope with one paw, which is also how an adult cat investigates any new, fairly small object. Lying in wait, chasing, stalking, the stalking run, and the pounce onto the prey appear in rapid succession. In the fourth week, the mother cat begins to carry dead prey into the nest, where the kittens watch her eat it. In the following weeks the kittens' reactions to the prey animal mature. These are completely developed by the time the mother cat brings the first live prey animals to the kittens, in about their sixth week. By this time the kittens have at their disposal all of the instinctive movements for catching prey. The killing bite is the last element to develop. This late development has survival value, for the kittens would surely injure one other while playing if the response developed earlier. As they play with the first live prey animals brought into the nest by the mother, the ordered sequence leading to the killing bite—lying in wait, stalking, pouncing, and seizing—establishes itself gradually.

Mother cats with kittens older than three weeks usually catch considerably more mice than usual, presumably for the benefit of the kittens who are now being weaned from breast milk to solid food. It is the behavior of the kittens themselves that stimulates the mother's hunting activity. From the fourth to the sixth weeks, when the mother brings dead prey animals to the nest, she growls to attract the attention of the kittens. The growling may change into a coaxing purr, and she will paw the dead animal several times before eating it, once she is certain that the kittens are watching. This very same behavior can be seen in domestic cats, even if they do not have kittens. They may catch a mouse, kill it, and then bring it to the feet of the human companion, who in this instance is serving as a substitute kitten. Males as well as females behave in this manner. It is less important for the human to congratulate the cat than it is simply to approach the cat and look at what he or she caught.

However, the mother cat does not teach the killing bite but rather elicits it by her behavior or from the behavior of a littermate. The mother brings into the nest a live prey animal and releases it. She swiftly catches the released animal as the kittens observe her. They do not learn from her example, as one would imagine; she appeals to their sense of competition as they eventually try to beat her to the mouse during the several times she releases it. The released mouse triggers the kittens' prey-catching activity by running away, and its swift recapture by the older cat compels the kittens to be even quicker if they want to catch it before their mother seizes it again. It looks like a game but is in fact a serious lesson. It is important to note that the keenest domestic cats never seize their prey with as much wild eagerness and determination as young male wild cats. (This is what makes domestic cats suitable as pets.) Yet the instinct to kill prey can be observed by the ninth week in domestic kittens.

If the mother cat does not bring live prey to the kittens during the critical period between their sixth and about their twentieth weeks, the kittens either do not kill prey later in life or else learn to do so slowly and laboriously.

The development of the killing bite is connected with the growth of the canine teeth, which are the ones employed for this purpose. The deciduous or milk teeth are all in place by the fifth week and ready to function. During the transition from deciduous to permanent teeth there may be one or two weeks when the temporary canines are too weak to function and the permanent ones are not yet long enough. This happens sometime between the fourth and sixth months. In a natural setting, the litter of kittens breaks up as a family by the sixth month. This happily coincides with the development of all the permanent teeth.

All cats, both young and old, engage in play activity. Much of this play behavior is connected in one way or another with prey-catching activity. Cats tend to play with their captured prey both before and after they have killed it. But there is also true play, which cats indulge in *without* prey animals and which some cat owners refer to as the "nightly crazies." In such play the normally quiet animal suddenly dashes across the room in a crouched position. All elements of prey capture can be seen, including stalking, watching posture, creeping, pouncing, seizing with the teeth, carrying around, and tossing objects away. During the crazies, the cat or kitten may expend more energy than if he were actually hunting. To the novice cat owner this is a startling and perplexing set of behaviors. It is probably safe to assume that all cat play mimics the dynamics of cat existence from prey capture to declarations of dominance to fighting over females and territory. It is harmless, fascinating and, more often than not, quite funny if not outright laughable.

MATING

To the uninitiated, feline sexuality comes as a rude and often disturbing surprise. Feline sexual behaviors create the impression of pain, trauma, and uncontrollable body malfunction. However, neither male nor female cats are sick or in pain when they lock into the extraordinary behaviors associated with the mating process. It only appears that way.

Domestic female cats may have as many as four or more cycles of estrus (heat) throughout the year, unless they become pregnant or are neutered. Male cats mate at any time of the year if they are stimulated by the presence of a female in heat. Cats become capable of mating between six and eighteen months, depending on the breed, the individual cat, the conditions of the environment, and the amount of stimulation from other cats. In the female, estrus typically lasts between five and eight days but can range from three to twenty days. Some experts believe mating shortens the duration of the estrus period; others believe it has no bearing on it at all.

A female in heat behaves at first in an unusually affectionate manner, rubbing against furniture, carpeting, and human legs. As estrus progresses, she may emit low and throaty sounds that can be disturbing. These noises are meant to attract male cats. The male responds by spraying sexually scented urine against walls and other vertical objects and by acting aggressively toward other cats. They also make a great effort to get outdoors to find the female. Male cats (and females as well) are better off being surgically neutered within the first year to avoid these behaviors as well as unwanted pregnancies.

The Social Life of Cats

What is it that enables a creature of solitude and extreme independence to share its existence with humans and other animals? It is quite likely that we humans encourage and maintain juvenile tendencies and childlike dependency in our pets, starting in kittenhood. Despite the loss of savage wildness and the exchange of total independence for domestic comforts and safety, the typical house cat cannot escape the matrix of feline behavior. A cat is always a cat, whether it's living in a split-level ranch home, a twenty-story apartment house, or a mountain crevice, taking the afternoon sun along the timberline. Relations with other cats in or out of its own territory remain unchanged in format if not in intensity.

A chance encounter. When two strange cats meet, which almost never happens in the wild (except for mating), they cautiously sniff each other. At first, they sniff each other's noses, although they do not actually touch. The whiskers act as feelers as they size up each other's napes and flanks and ultimately smell each other's anuses. Although there is a slight resistance to this aspect of the investigation, one finally allows the other to continue sniffing, provided the encounter remains friendly. Very often, the friendliness ends when one moves a bit too quickly while examining the nape of the neck. Defensive postures quickly develop, and one or both begin to hiss. From there the more assertive of the two will deliver a blow on the nose with his paw and send his opponent running. This automatically establishes a kind of social structure, with one cat dominant over the other. The encounter may repeat itself several times before the confrontation ends. Depending on the territoriality of the dominant cat, things may go very sour and result in a direct attack. This is highly likely if both cats are whole tomcats. The cat that is on his own territory is usually the dominant animal, at least in the beginning. In variations of this behavior, both animals will crouch, staring at each other for long periods. Extremely timid cats will run and hide as long as there is a strange cat in their territory.

Physical clash. Adult male cats are the most likely to fight one another. However, all cats, including females and those that have been neutered, are capable of fighting with one another. Young cats are the least likely to engage in serious fights, although kittenish play is a foreshadowing of future aggressive behavior. Kittens fighting are amusing to watch because their technique is clumsy and because the battle seems more like play than combat.

You must take cat fights seriously and avoid them at all costs because of the potential dangers involved to the adversaries and to innocent bystanders. When cats fight, they do not have in their repertoire of behavior a gesture for submission as do dogs, wolves, and other mammals. This leaves a losing cat with no reasonable means of surrender and release from the fight. His only chance is to escape if possible. Frequently the winner chases the loser and brings him down once again. Serious injury is a certainty, and in some situations the fight may continue to the death or close to it. Veterinarians are at times called upon to tend seriously injured cats, with part of an ear or tail bitten off or a large abscess festering on the back of the neck.

A clowder of cats. The factors that permit cats to get along with one another are not entirely understood by researchers. Many experienced cat owners and breeders have perfectly delightful stories of cats that spend entire lifetimes together in peace and harmony. However, the dominance of one cat over another is usually subtle in manner and sometimes imperceptible to the enthusiastic cat lover, who translates animal actions into human terms. The use of the food bowls and the litter box by a dominant cat can act as a guide to the degree of harmony in a multicat home. In some hierarchical structures, a top cat emerges, along with one or more low cats on the totem pole who behave in a cowering manner to all the others. One can never predict with certainty how the social structure will develop between cats. It depends on the individual character of each of the animals involved. In some feline communities, there are dominant cats, cats of lower rank, and even one or more social outcasts.

When two or more cats share a territory or a common home, they may become completely accustomed to one another, without much need for the violent fights that cats are capable of engaging in. However, a strange cat entering that established society would certainly be examined and quite likely attacked. At the very least, one or more cats may express their dismay by urinating and defecating outside their litter boxes.

Because domestic cats do not choose their primary territory but rather have it selected for them by humans, they seem to accept one another with much greater ease than their wild cousins. This is an extremely important aspect of domesticity. The denial of the primary decision in a cat's life probably has a subordinating effect. This may be what allows them to share a territory in domesticity with one or more cats.

Cat owners can greatly enhance their own and their cats' lifestyles by understanding and accepting the basics of cat behavior. The importance of territory applies to such everyday elements as feeding dishes, litter boxes, resting areas, toys, and hiding places. Allowing for predatory behavior, if only in the manner of play, is extremely important for the mental health of a house cat. Do not discourage prey capture in any form unless it is destructive to the home or someone living in it. Sexual behavior cannot be avoided unless the animal is surgically sterilized, and even then not all of it can be eliminated. Matters of dominance, social harmony, and aggressiveness must be dealt with sympathetically.

Sensory Messages

Even a kitten can communicate its instinctive needs and urges with the sensory tools with which it was born. In addition to their other uses, these tools are used for communicating with other cats and humans; they are components of the feline catalog of basic behaviors. A cat's primary means of communication are vocalization, the primary senses, and body language.

Vocalization

The most obvious form of communication is vocalization. The repertoire of feline vocalization includes chirping (a happy greeting); a demanding meow or *mrwowl* (indicating complaining, begging, or sexual arousal); crying, shrieking, or yowling (indicating pain, confusion, disorientation, or a great dissatisfaction); growling, snarling, hissing, or making spitting sounds (a warning, often of impending aggression); and the open-mouthed meow without a sound (a delicate, diplomatic demand or complaint).

The large cats of the jungles and plains are the greatest of the vocalizers, but do not underestimate the domestic cat's powerful ability to manifest its roar. Vocalizing occurs between rival males when competing for a female in heat. There is much vocalization when two males are about to fight for territory. It is also an announcement of a cat's presence in its own territory. In the plains and the jungles and the deserts, wherever cats roam, their distant roars and close meows seem like a lonely, haunting sound directed toward the sky, but they are in fact a declaration of existence aimed at all those near and far. When your kitten looks at you and meows, it either wants to be fed, to be petted, or to declare its presence in your life. Consider the meow a little mighty roar.

The Primary Senses

Eyes. Cat eyes are extraordinary even more for their special abilities than for their good looks. The eyes of the cat are dramatically large and reflect how important vision is for these animals. In daylight cats possess about the same visual sharpness as humans. However, cats have about six times the sensitivity of humans to low light levels, allowing their eyes to adjust to sudden darkness faster than ours.

Inside and to the rear of the eye is the retina, which receives light and sends it to the brain as vision. Behind the retina is a layer of cells known as the *tapetum lucidum*. Its function is to reflect any light not absorbed during its first passage through the retina. This second pass of low light allows cats to see clearly in near darkness, which is when your kitty usually goes on the hunt for its prey. When you see your cat's eyes glow in the dark, it is the reflection of light striking the iridescent cells of the tapetum lucidum.

Ears. The cat's ability to hear is far superior to the hearing of humans, even that of young children. The highest hearing range for humans is twenty kilocycles. Cats can hear between fifty to sixty kilocycles. They are capable of capturing sounds from the environment of which humans are never aware. They can hear the distant movement and vocal squeaks of mice and isolate them from other sounds, even if they come from behind the walls of your home. This may explain why they often ignore humans who speak to them. They may simply be distracted by something else they hear.

Nose. Although the nose is part of the respiratory system, it also houses the olfactory nerves providing the sense of smell, which is an essential means of receiving information. The sense of smell is an important tool for protection and influences a cat's appetite and many aspects of its behavior. Cats can smell better than humans but not as well as dogs.

Body Language

At times a cat uses the way it positions its body to communicate specific messages to friend, foe, or loved one. A cat's body language has many gestures and positions in its inventory, such as the tilt of its head, the position of the tail and ears, and facial expressions. These are all meant to communicate either aggression, pleasure, sexual inclination, hunger, dominance, or the claiming of territory. The most obvious body gestures are those of the fight-or-flight stance—the coat spiking out to look bigger in front of an enemy, the Halloweenlike arching of the back, the erect ears rolled back, the whiskers forward, the eyes squinting, and the forward motion in a sideways stance.

When a cat is frightened, it may take a crouched position with its paws tucked under its body. Its ears and whiskers flatten out and its eyes will open wider as it spits, hisses, and maybe even drools.

A cat that is on the hunt is a sight to behold. All four legs bend to place the body in an extreme crouched position as the cat hugs the ground in an effort to avoid having its presence detected. All cats, especially wild cats, do this. It is part of the stalking, ambush, and pounce mechanism of prey capture. Eyes open wider than usual, and ears and whiskers push forward from the head. It is quite an intense and frightening sight if you are the quarry.

A cat that cuddles in your lap with its eyes half closed, that purrs a rubbery rasp from within is telling you something about contentment and satisfaction with the status quo. It is saying that it's stress-free and at peace. It is also taking a nap in comfort and doesn't want to be disturbed.

Cats like to circle around the legs of humans and rub their faces and bodies against them. This is called *bunting behavior* and is a physical means of transferring the cat's scent onto the human. It is probably another way of marking territory. What is actually happening is that the cat is transferring scent to the human body with glandular secretions from its own facial area, when head butting, or from the glands in its tail, when winding between a human's legs.

The cat's tail is in most cases long and graceful, although in some breeds it is short and stumpy. Many cat experts believe that the tail gives the cat's body balance when it is running and jumping. More than that, though, it communicates to all its emotional state and pending actions. A cat, for example, that releases a mouse and watches it run usually flicks its tail back and forth, indicating that it will run after the doomed prey animal and will pounce on it. A tail that is held straight up usually indicates a pleasant, happy state of mind. When the tail bangs on the floor or on your lap, back and forth, your pet is signaling irritation; it's best to stop what you're doing. When the hairs on the tail puff outward, the cat is either frightened or in an aggressive mode. When a cat tucks its tail between its legs, as dogs do at times, it is indicating a submissive frame of mind and is either protecting its genitals or making itself as small as possible.

These feline basic behaviors serve as the idiom of the cat. Since our young kittens and mature cats have no spoken language, this is their means of communication in order to get what they require. It only seems illogical at times because some of their behavior is incongruous with the human sensibility. Pet kittens do not really need to hunt, since they are well cared for by their human families. Nevertheless, the instinct to hunt remains. The same is true for the behaviors associated with claiming and protecting territory. A cat that feels threatened or upset for any reason, real or imagined, will urinate and defecate outside its litter box in totally unexpected places that are never desirable. It is important to understand and be patient with a kitten's seemingly disturbing behavior. Your insight into feline nature will make such behavior easier to cope with and redirect in some way.

SEVEN

GROOMING YOUR KITTEN

Kittens can give you a complex, because unlike the rest of us, they continually wash themselves. They do it by licking their coats. For the areas they cannot reach with their tongue, they lick a paw and then use the paw as a wash cloth. They keep themselves very clean, unless of course they get into something and then they need your help. No matter how clean kittens are, they can use some help if their sumptuous fur coats get dry, dirty, matted, tangled, pinched, smeared, stained, greasy, or just clumpy-looking. If a kitten fails to preen himself, it may be a sign of illness.

It's important to understand that grooming does more than keep your kitten looking good. A kitten looks good when he is healthy, and health is maintained with good food, exercise, medical attention, play, a happy home, and of course regular grooming. When you groom him properly, you are actually practicing preventive medicine. As you brush your kitten or trim his nails, you are incidentally examining his body. It is a way to detect potential problems that can seriously affect your kitten's health. In the course of grooming, you can examine your kitten from nose to tail and look for fleas, lumps under the skin, infections, rashes, dental problems, and even minor injuries. Combing and brushing down to the skin enables you to render an in-depth examination, the kind a veterinarian may give him.

Grooming primarily refers to maintaining his coat (daily), trimming his nails (once a week), cleaning his ears and eyes (as needed), cleaning his teeth (as needed), and giving your kitten a bath (as needed). Some long-coated cats may require a bit of scissoring here and there if the coat gets raggedy-looking. You may choose to leave that to a professional groomer.

Because the vast majority of people who live with a kitten are only interested in those things that make cats good companions, they have no need for show grooming techniques. Only those grooming needs that pertain to good health and an attractive appearance are presented here.

Coat Care

Adult cats seldom sit still for combing, brushing, or bathing if it isn't part of an established routine. The feline mind depends on patterns of behavior, theirs and yours, as a matter of instinct. Few cats like surprises or unexpected activities. This preference is tied in with matters of survival, hunting, and territory. When it comes to grooming, it is a great idea to begin brushing your kitten every day as part of a ritual even if it isn't really necessary. Making it an acceptable activity is a matter of associations, so connect these activities in the kitten's mind with something expected and very pleasant.

First, select a grooming place and a grooming time and stick to it. A table top, a kitchen counter, any surface including your lap is fine. In order to create pleasant associations, do not begin grooming right away. Take the kitten to the grooming place at the established time and just let him become familiar with it as you pet him, say loving things, and even offer him a toy. The next day, bring him back and make a fuss over him again, only this time spread out all your grooming tools for him to sniff, walk over, and examine. Allow him to sit on the brush if he wants, lick the comb if that's his desire, and push the nail trimmer around with his paws. He'll soon tire of this and walk away. On the third day repeat the routine only gently and, without fanfare, begin brushing him.

The most important aspect of grooming, as it applies to hygiene and good looks, is daily brushing (and combing for long and medium-long coats). You may do this every day, in the same place at the same time, to give the kitten a good appearance as well as to avoid the ill effects of the animal's constant self-grooming. Cats continually lick their coats clean with their tongues. As they do this, they swallow a great deal of their own hair. After a while the hair accumulates in a mass in the digestive system and develops into entwined ropes or *hairballs*. These eventually cause blockages along the digestive tract. Most hairballs are eventually passed through, some are expelled by regurgitation, and in rare cases they must be removed surgically. Brushing and combing your kitten every day will definitely help prevent this problem.

Short-haired coat. A short-haired kitten with a smooth coat does not require a great deal of coat care. Bear in mind, the object of brushing is to remove dead and loose hair as often as you can. A short-haired cat with coarse hair will probably have an abundance of dead hair to remove and will require more time. *Never lose sight of the fact that your kitten's skin is thin and tender and requires a soft, gentle approach to combing and brushing.*

It is not a good idea to brush the coat when it is dry. Moisten the coat before starting out with a small spritz of commercial coat conditioner or plain water; spray it onto your hands; rub it over the entire body with your fingers as though giving a very gentle massage. Once you have *slightly* moistened the coat, use your soft natural-bristle brush. As the kitten matures, you may use a hard rubber brush (a curry brush) or even a bent-wire slicker brush. If your kitten rejects being brushed, bribe him with a food treat.

As you brush your kitten, imagine you're giving him a sensuous back-scratching, the kind that makes your eyes close with pleasure. Work the soft brush through the coat with long, gentle strokes, taking as much dead and loose hair with you as possible. Pull it off the brush as it accumulates. Be sure to stroke the entire body from shoulder to toes, from nose to tail. Work the brush gently but with the necessary pressure to move the hair in whichever direction you're going. Each brush stroke should be part of a steady, rhythmical movement that is comfortable for you and the kitten.

Some short coats consist of a single coat, and others consist of a double coat. The single coat is sleek and shiny and has a delicate texture. It lies flat against the skin. The double coat has long hairs on the outside that display the color and pattern and a short, fluffy, dense coat on the belly. Double-coated cats tend to shed more. Daily brushing, massaging, and combing are important.

After brushing, run a comb through the coat, starting at the head and working to the tail, in the natural direction of the growth. Brush the stomach, legs, tail, and head as well as the main part of the coat. Afterward you may use a commercial coat conditioner or dressing, but that is optional. Finish the session with a single-coated kitten by polishing the coat with a chamois cloth. All short-coated cats should look smooth and shiny. All double-coated cats should look soft and luxurious.

Long-haired coat. As with the short coat, moisten the coat before starting the daily combing and brushing routine. Do not groom a dry coat. Spritz a small amount of coat conditioner or plain water on to your hands; rub it over the entire body with your fingers as though giving a very gentle massage. Once you have *slightly* moistened the coat, you may begin the grooming process. *Never lose sight of the fact that your kitten's skin is thin and tender and requires a soft, gentle approach to combing and brushing.*

Long to medium-long coats should generally be combed first (with a half-fine half-medium comb) and then brushed. The main point to combing any coat type is to remove mats and tangles and smooth out the coat. Combing also helps remove dirt and dead hair. A professional groomer's trick for making this task easier is to use a cream rinse during the final stages of a bath.

Starting with the trunk, comb the longest hair with the medium-tooth portion of the comb. Work upward and outward as you stroke the back, sides, and behind the legs. Get the teeth deep into the hair, close to the skin, and carefully lift upward as you comb the fur out. Do not forget to comb the flanks, belly, and entire leg areas. Take the end of the tail in your fingers and shake it carefully. Use the medium-tooth portion of the comb for the tail and groom with the lay of the fur.

The fine-tooth portion of the comb should be used on the forehead and around the ears in an upward and forward direction; cheek hair should be guided forward and outward.

Comb the feet and the legs with the fine-tooth portion of the combination comb. Stroke the protruding leg hair in an upward direction. Comb the long tufts of fur between the toes upward with the fine teeth.

As a final step, use a soft, natural-bristle brush to gently stroke with the lay of the fur, using short movements, from the shoulder to the haunch to the tail. The brush should catch any remaining dead hair while applying the finishing touches.

Daily combing and brushing will help prevent tangles, knots, and mats in the fur of the long-haired kitten. The amount of matting depends on the texture and length of the fur. Coarse hair, for example, will not mat as readily as fine hair. There are several detangling liquids available, to be used in conjunction with the fine teeth of your comb or other detangling tool, that make mat removal much easier.

As you brush, use the necessary pressure to move the hair in whichever direction you're going, but continue to be gentle. Swing your hand, wrist, and entire arm in whatever direction you're brushing with a long, stroking movement. Each brush stroke should be part of a steady, rhythmical movement that is comfortable for you and the cat. If you use a steady, sweeping motion, you can brush your kitten without tiring for as long as it takes to do a thorough job.

Shedding

There is always falling hair in the house whether you live with an American Shorthair or a Persian. Shedding is the natural process of casting off one layer of the hair coat and replacing it with another. With fur-covered animals such as the cat, nature's purpose is to replace the heavy winter coat with a lighter summer one. As the weather becomes colder, a heavier coat grows once again. It is mostly a matter of insulation.

Shedding the winter coat begins in the spring and under

normal conditions takes approximately three weeks. Shedding the summer coat and replacing it with the heavier winter *pelage* occurs in autumn, preparing the animal for cold weather. Some breeds shed just once a year in a long cycle that achieves the same effect. Many researchers believe that shedding is influenced by the length of time spent outdoors exposed to the natural sequences of light and darkness. Shedding and regrowth begin in spring as the days get longer and again in late summer as they shorten. In the natural state, animals are never exposed to any strong light other than daylight, and their coats conform to seasonal variations involving day-to-night ratios. It is theorized that abnormal shedding cycles may be caused by a pet cat's indoor life, which involves arrhythmic exposure to light and darkness. Pets exposed to prolonged periods of electric lights may have extended shedding cycles and shed continuously.

Nothing will prevent a cat from shedding. All you can do is try to reduce the impact. Cats require a well-balanced diet, as found in premium commercial cat food. If your cat is shedding excessively, perhaps a change of diet is called for. If the cat is fed home-cooked meals, a high-quality vitamin and mineral supplement is necessary along with a commercial coat conditioner or a teaspoonful a day of animal fat (cooked or raw). These supplements may be necessary even if your cat is being fed an acceptable diet. Artificial heat can also enhance the shedding process: if your kitten has taken to sleeping on a hot radiator, shoo him off. Regular combing and brushing help rid any cat or kitten of dead hair and loose dander.

Shedding can be minimized, though not totally eliminated, by giving your cat a hot-to-warm-water bath and a thorough comb-out. Use a cream rinse for long-coated cats or cats with a dense undercoat. After the bath, towel the excess water off the cat's body. Next, use a warm-air blow dryer for as long as it takes to dry the coat. Use the lowest setting and move the blow dryer back and forth along the cat's coat, but do not get it too close. As you blow-dry, comb out the coat vigorously. The comb must penetrate down to the skin on all parts of the body. The warm air will force out onto your comb most of the dead hair, the dying hair, and the loose hair. The hair that you remove with this technique is the hair that would have been shed in your house over a long period of time. Do this twice a year, just as the coat is about to fall off.

Mats, Knots, and Tangles

The outer layer of each individual cat hair is formed by overlapping scales. These scales protect the inner structure. However, the ends of the scales protrude and form microscopic barbs. When there is a lack of oil on the surface of the hair shaft or if it is exceptionally dry, these barbs tend to lock into one another and create the mats, tangles, and knots that are so troublesome. Mats are also formed by an accumulation of static electricity along the barbed edges.

Commercially manufactured tangle removers are formulated with oils that are antistatic in nature while they add body to the hair. They also help repair the damaged hair caused by the tangles while helping reduce the incidence of matting. The manufacturer's directions should be followed for good results. Be sure to drench the matted surfaces with the tangle-removing liquid. Use the fluid as a lubricant for the locked barbs by rubbing it in thoroughly. Allow the product to remain on the coat until the hair is damp or almost dry; then begin detangling with a detangling tool, or your thumb and index finger. It is best to remove tangles and mats before bathing your kitten or adult cat.

Be on the lookout for matting during periods of damp weather. If the kitten gets out in the rain or snow, heaven forbid, its long hair is quite likely to mat. Wet hair will tangle if not cared for properly.

GROOMING TOOLS

- **Natural-bristle brush**. The one grooming tool needed by everyone for the care of long-, medium-, and short-coated cats. All bristle brushes come in a variety of sizes and shapes, with soft, medium, or stiff bristles. Select one based on your cat's age, size, and coat. Common sense will guide you. The best brushes have all-natural bristles.
- **Fine-wire slicker brush.** Rectangular in shape, with a wooden handle. Slicker brushes are short with bent-wire teeth placed closely together, resembling the metal fins inside an air conditioner. Their purpose is to untangle mats and remove dead hair.
- **Hard rubber brush.** Made of one molded piece of rubber that includes the teeth. This brush is for grooming and polishing short-coated and smooth-coated cats. It is also good for shampooing and massaging without scratching a kitten's sensitive skin. It is of no use for long- or medium-coated cats.
- **Chamois cloth.** For polishing a single-, short-coated cat after brushing. Some coats are too fine for brushing, and a wipe with a chamois adds the finishing touch. A silk scarf or piece of velvet will also provide the necessary luster when rubbed into the coat.
- **Half-medium, half-fine comb.** The most useful comb to own because it can be used for most

breeds and coat types. The fine teeth are for soft or silky hair; the medium teeth are for coats of average texture. Both medium and fine teeth are often used on different sections of the same cat's coat. The size of the comb and the tooth length to get depend on the length of your cat's coat. A long or medium coat requires longer teeth. Blunt teeth on the comb are necessary for all short-coated cats.

- **Medium Belgium comb with a handle.** Very useful for grooming long-haired cats. The handle makes lifting the coat, layer by layer, easier to accomplish. The ends of the teeth should be rounded so they do not cause scratches or skin irritation.

Trimming Your Kitten's Nails

You should trim your kitten's nails once a week, just before a grooming session *and definitely before a bath*. It is best to get your kitten used to nail trimming as soon as possible because adult cats resist the procedure unless they have been exposed to it at an early age. Trimming your kitten's nails helps prevent destructive behavior toward your furniture and injury to humans and other pets.

Feline nails are unique because they are retractable and most of the time do not show. They are usually withdrawn and tucked into and between the paw pads. When cats walk, only the very tips come in contact with the ground. The nails are formidable weapons that extend when the cat prepares to fight, run, or climb. A kitten or adult cat will unsheathe its nails when it is frightened or panicked. Tree climbing, jumping, escape maneuvers, playing, fighting, mating, and many other activities involve the exposure of the cat's nails. Of course, unsheathed nails are necessary for catching prey animals. They are indispensable, which is why the strictly enforced policy of the Cat Fanciers' Association is to forbid the surgical procedure of removing the nails (*declawing*) and not register a declawed cat or allow it to enter a cat show. The CFA believes the procedure is inhumane, disfigures cats, and is not in their best interests.

When a kitten uses his nails on a scratching post or your furniture, he is obeying an instinctive impulse to remove the outer layer of the tissue and make room for the continuously growing nail underneath. You can avoid much of the damage to yourself and your possessions by keeping the nails trimmed.

How to trim. The trick to trimming your kitten's nails is getting him to extend them out of the skin covering, between the pads. This is accomplished by applying gentle pressure with your fingers on the paw pads where the nails are retracted. Place the kitten's paw on your open palm. Select a nail and press your thumb against the corresponding toe. The nail will appear. If the nails are a quarter inch past the pink area, they should be clipped. Most cat nails are white or buff-colored at the tips and pink as they get closer to the base. The pink area is called the *quick*; it indicates where the nerve endings are located and where the blood vessels begin. You must never clip the nails at the quick. If you do, you will cause pain and slight bleeding, and possibly infection. In dark-haired cats, some or all of the nails may be black or darker than usual. This will make it difficult to see the quick. If you trim the nail just at the curve, you will avoid any mistakes. If the procedure is too nerve-wracking for you, take the cat to a professional groomer or veterinarian and watch how he or she does it.

Once the nails have been snipped with the cutting tool, it

is a good idea to smooth down the sharp edges of each nail as you would when cutting your own nails, with an emery board and nail buffer. Some cat owners use the emery board exclusively as a way of keeping the nails in trim. Although this procedure is time consuming, it does work. When clipping the nails, always use a nail trimmer that was designed especially for cats. These vital tools are readily available in a pet supply store.

Ears

Kittens do not require any involved ear care other than an occasional cleaning and inspection. However, cats and older kittens should have their ears routinely cleaned with a few drops of light mineral oil or a feline ear-cleaning product prepared specifically for this purpose. Moisten the inside of the ear with a few drops of the mineral oil or feline ear solution. Experienced cat owners then swab out the liquid with a cotton swab (Q-tip) but a finger-held cotton ball is suggested for the novice. Do not enter the ear canal too deeply with either material for fear of damaging the delicate hearing mechanism.

If your kitten does not accept ear cleaning very well, have someone help you. Wrap the cat's body in a towel so that all four paws are restrained and have your assistant hold him firmly. Only the head should extend out of the towel. Proceed with the ear cleaning. If there is a great accumulation of ear wax, do not attempt to clean it out yourself unless you are very experienced. Occasional ear cleaning is more for the sake of hygiene than good looks. It helps prevent costly and persistent ear conditions.

Be sure that your pet does not suffer from ear mites, which are common in kittens and some grown cats. Constant wiping or scratching at the ears with the paws is a sure sign of mites, as is a chronic shaking of the head. Look inside the ear for redness due to inflammation and a black caking or crusting. If you see these symptoms, take your cat to a veterinarian for examination and treatment.

Eyes

With the exception of tear staining on the facial coat, eye care is not really a grooming issue, nor does it require any serious involvement for kittens. Healthy eyes are bright and lustrous. When something is medically wrong, the eyes become watery, inflamed, and even infected. The *haw* or third lid closes laterally in some types of eye problems and makes the eye appear covered with a translucent film. Medicated eye solution for cats or boric acid solution can be dropped or wiped into the eyes, but a visit to the veterinarian is the most prudent move.

Long-haired cats, particularly those with short, snub noses (Persian types), tend to weep frequently, possibly because the tear ducts are compressed. The discharge of tears eventually causes eye stain, a dark brownish look to the fur on the inner side of the eyes. When the tears overflow, they eventually cake on the facial hair. With such cats, daily care is absolutely necessary. You may clean the area below the eye with a commercial feline eye solution available in pet supply stores. This will remove any dirt that may be the cause of the tearing. Wash the stained area with a cotton ball soaked with warm water and dry it thoroughly with a dry cotton ball. Stubborn stains can be covered with a commercial eye stain remover, available as a white powder or a silicone chalk stick. Professional groomers may choose to scissor away the discolored hair.

Teeth

Much dental work performed by veterinarians would be unnecessary if the kitten owner took proper care. Tartar accumulates constantly in the cat's mouth and should be removed on a regular basis to prevent mouth odor, gum disease, and loss of teeth. It is very difficult to clean the teeth of an adult cat. A veterinarian is usually needed for this chore, and the cat must be anesthetized. To avoid this hassle, start cleaning your kitten's teeth early in the game so that he will happily adjust to the process.

Practice good dental hygiene once a week, or more, with a toothbrush or device designed for cleaning a cat's teeth. You can also use a soft baby toothbrush or a cotton swab or even a washcloth dipped in a paste of warm water and table salt or baking soda. However, brushes manufactured for cat teeth are best. They are available in pet supply stores and mail-order catalogs along with very fine no-foam toothpastes formulated for cats. *Never use human toothpaste* for cats, especially kittens. It foams a great deal and is almost traumatic for your pet. It also contains fluoride, which can be medically harmful to small animals.

A cat's teeth are most affected by the quality of his diet and your diligent cleaning practices, just as for humans. A sound diet from a premium commercial cat food contributes much to maintaining healthy teeth. Tartar accumulations can also be retarded by introducing a small quantity of dry, hard food into the diet. The abrasion against the teeth and gums caused by chewing helps.

The Bath

The most frequently asked question on this subject is "How often?" The answer you get depends on whom you ask. Breeders who show pedigreed cats bathe them before every show. A professional groomer may tell you that it is best to give a bath approximately every six weeks. Experienced pet owners will tell you that they only bathe their cats when they look dirty. There are cat owners who never bathe their cats.

Consider this. An occasional cat bath is not only an aesthetic consideration but one of health as well. A now-and-again bath plus daily brushing and combing helps prevent unhealthy hairballs from forming along the cat's digestive tract. It also goes a long way toward fighting the millions of opportunistic bacteria that live on the bodies of all mammals, just waiting for a way around the immune system. It is true that a bath will invigorate the skin and rid the body of dead hair and debris as well as remove unnecessary oil. However, too many baths tend to dry out the skin and the coat. Some professionals believe that short-coated cats can be bathed twice a year and long-coated cats can be bathed about every two months. Still, there are many who believe a cat should only be bathed when absolutely necessary, when he has gotten into something that makes him unpleasing to be around. Your future experience with your kitten will help you set your own guidelines.

Ideally, the habit of bathing a cat should begin while he is a kitten so that he will adapt to and accept the process with ease and security. Most cats do not enjoy getting wet and will resist unless they've been exposed to the experience early in life. When a cat becomes attached to one or two humans in his life, he will generally allow them to do *most* things necessary for his well-being, such as giving medicine, trimming his nails, and giving him a bath. If you wait too long beyond kittenhood, he may resist a bath by scratching you and trying to get away. However, since most kittens are treated with love and affection and are constantly being held, they do submit to a bath and wait patiently for it to be over.

What You Will Need to Bathe Your Kitten Successfully

- Commercial shampoo formulated for cats only (Cat shampoos are labeled for specific purposes that are self-explanatory—tearless, medicated, for fleas and ticks, with conditioner, for color coats, for white coats, etc.)
- Small sink or plastic tub (A double kitchen sink or two tubs are best—one for soapy water, the second for rinsing.)
- Small window screen (for front paw traction)
- Bath mat or folded dish towel (for hind paw traction)
- Spray hose (optional)
- Large plastic cup
- Detangling liquid (for cats with matted hair)
- Mineral oil (for the eyes)
- Cotton balls (for the ears)
- Cat comb (half fine/half medium)
- Natural-bristle brush
- Rubber brush (for short-haired coats)
- Electric hair dryer (hand-held)
- Three large towels
- Cat carrier (for confinement during drying)

Prebath Requirements

- Trim your kitten's nails.
- Comb and brush out the coat, removing loose or dead hair; remove all mats and tangles. If necessary, use a commercial detangling liquid.
- Place a few drops of mineral oil in the kitten's eyes with a dropper to prevent burning caused by shampoo.
- Put absorbent cotton in each ear canal to prevent water from running in.
- Have someone your kitten likes present to assist you for the first few baths.
- Use your kitchen or bathroom sink. A double kitchen sink is most useful.
- Fill the sink one third with lukewarm water and a small quantity of shampoo to begin cleaning the paws. If you have a double sink, fill one with clear water for rinsing.
- Lean the window screen against the side of the sink, allowing the kitten to cling to it with his front paws. Use a bath mat or folded towel for his hind paws.
- One person gives the bath while the other holds the kitten in place.

How to Bathe Your Kitten

The soak cycle. Fill the sink one-third full with warm water and add a capful of shampoo to it. The shampoo in the water makes it easier to wet down the coat as well as thoroughly clean between the toes. Place your kitten in the sink and put his front paws on the screen and his hind paws on the bath mat. Use the plastic cup to pour the soapy water gently over the cat. If there are no fleas to deal with, do not wet his head or face until last. However, wet the head first if the kitten is infested with any form of parasite. Otherwise, when the body becomes wet, the fleas will scurry to the head and ears, making it more difficult to get at them.

The wash cycle. If there are no fleas, work from back to front because wetting the head can be frightening to a cat. Talk to your kitten in a quiet, soothing, affectionate tone of voice as you work. The kitten may be somewhat calm by the time you start to pour water very gently on his head. Once all the fur is thoroughly wet, apply the cat shampoo, rubbing it in with your fingertips. Get it all the way down to the skin and clean the body with a massaging action, much as you would shampoo your own head. Be gentle, though. Once the body, legs, and tail are lathered, you may wet the head; use a tearless shampoo for that area no matter what kind of shampoo you use for the rest of the body.

Work up a good lather, getting it deep into the coat and onto the skin. Massage the shampoo into the shoulders, down the back and legs, between the toes, up and on the underbody, and finally along the tail. Gently scrub the head and the ears with your fingers. Carefully wash his face (avoiding the eyes), under his chin, and down his neck onto his chest. When a cat stands in bath water with a little shampoo added to it, the paws are automatically being softened and cleaned, especially between the toes. If the paws are sore or afflicted with a fungus or other irritation, use a medicated cat shampoo in the bath water.

The rinse cycle. Although your large plastic cup is adequate for rinsing, a hand spray or portable shower connected to the faucet is the most thorough way to rinse away the shampoo, dirt, and dead hair and skin. The cup will require much more effort. Either way, do not use the hand spray on the cat's head or face. It is kinder to use the cup.

Rinse from head to tail. Start at the head and go down the back to the sides of the body, and then the legs. That way all the soapy, dirty water runs off the cat and does not simply pour onto another part of the body.

If the kitten is very dirty, a second shampoo is desirable and should be given immediately. Do not shampoo twice unless it is absolutely necessary. Never keep a cat in water longer than necessary. He will become very fussy and try to bolt. He could also fall victim to a chill, which will cause medical problems. Young kittens are especially vulnerable to chills.

If you are using a double sink, now is the time to use the other side. Rinse the kitten thoroughly. Remove all the shampoo from the body or there will remain a dull, soapy residue. Then empty the sink, rinse it, and refill it with clear, tepid water. Rinse the kitten once more until you see clear water coming off the body. Take a large towel and blot the body dry to get rid of the excess water. Using a second towel, remove the little wet cat from the sink and place him on a dry counter. Towel-dry him instantly so he does not get chilled. With your fingers and the towel, gently squeeze the water out of the coat. Try not to create tangles during any part of the drying process. Continue to towel-dry until the cat is no longer dripping wet.

The blow-dry cycle. It is now time to use the portable hair dryer. Use it with the blower on but with the heat set on low. The high setting is too hot for cats. Never blow unheated air on the cat. For short-haired cats, use a soft, natural-bristle brush or rubber brush as you work with the dryer. The drying motion requires short, quick strokes with the brush and the dryer. For long-haired cats, apply a fluff-dry technique.

Do not let the warm air blow on the coat without using a natural-bristle brush or comb. Brush or comb the fur with long flowing strokes in an upward motion. This has the effect of lifting the hair and allowing its underside to dry from the flow of warm air. It also creates a very fluffy coat. Avoid blowing air directly into the kitten's face or ears or he will bolt.

The finish. Do not allow your squeaky-clean kitten to roam around the house while he is still damp. This will only get him dirty all over again. Line the bottom of your cat carrier with a clean towel and place him inside until he is mostly dry. Remember, long-haired cats will need more drying time than short-haired cats. Keep the carrier in a warm, safe area free from drafts and chills. Place it off the floor. This is very important.

When his coat is mostly dry, it is time to spray a coat conditioner on him, comb and brush him out, and tie a pretty ribbon around his neck. He now deserves a food treat for putting up with this disagreeable experience. And let him watch the birds from your living room window.

EIGHT

FEEDING THE KITTY

Who doesn't enjoy feeding kittens tidbits and table scraps by hand? There is nothing sweeter than smearing a bit of soft cooked meat on your finger and inviting the baby cat to lick it off. This is fine, providing it is just a treat and not the way you feed an entire meal to kitty. It is a fact that cats are carnivores and that meat is the major part of their diet, but there is more to their nutritional requirements than that. In order to grow properly and maintain the glow of good health, a kitten needs a complete and balanced diet. He must have the proper amounts of protein, carbohydrates, fat, vitamins, minerals, and water. Hand-fed or home-cooked meals may fill a kitten's belly but will probably leave him woefully lacking the nutrients for growth, health, and maintenance of muscles, bones, organs, blood, and the various chemical systems within the body.

Unless you have a technical grasp of your kitten's nutritional requirements, feeding him from your dinner plate, or even cooking for him, is hit or miss and usually inadequate. Feline nutritional needs are different from those of humans, dogs, and other animals, and it's important for pet owners to understand this.

Cats living in the wild must hunt to survive. They must continually move about their established territory if they are to remain close to their food source, which happens to be other animals that creep, crawl, run, swim, or fly. As solitary creatures, cats must stalk their prey, ambush it, and kill it. Once they have captured a prey animal, they systematically devour it. Even our own kitty cats do this. The first element consumed is the blood, an important source of nutrition. Next, they tear open the stomach and eat the partially digested vegetable matter. Unlike humans, cats instinctively eat what is best for them and consume all of the organs, including the liver, heart, kidneys, lungs, and intestines. Then they crush the bones and eat them, especially the marrow. Fatty meats, connective tissue, and lean muscle meat follow in quick succession.

Proteins and minerals are absorbed from the blood, bones, marrow, organs, and muscle meat. The vegetable matter in the stomach supplies vitamins and additional minerals. Cats obtain their required fat from the fatty meat and intestines, along with fatty acids, vitamins, and some carbohydrates. The hair supplies roughage, as do other indigestible elements, particularly from the vegetable contents. Cats also obtain vitamins and minerals from exposure to the sun and by drinking water, lots of water. In the wild, all cats benefit from a well-rounded nutritional menu provided by the prey animals they eat, and they derive all the positive effects possible from their diet, assuming they eat often enough.

If you carefully examine the ingredients on the label of a

premium commercial kitten or cat food, you will find approximately the same basic components as provided by a consumed prey animal with only a few exceptions. It is absolutely essential for all kittens and adult cats, even if they are pets, to achieve this same high level of nutritional balance in order to grow and maintain good health throughout their lives.

The Nuts and Bolts of Feline Nutrition

Energy

Like all mammals, cats use energy (fuel) to perform all body functions and activities whether asleep or awake. Energy is obtained from the burning of food consumed or the destruction of protein sources obtained from body tissue.

The energy requirements of cats vary. Size, age, activity, state of health, and the indoor or outdoor temperature influence these requirements. The energy requirement of a cat per unit of body weight decreases as the cat's weight increases. This means a small kitten requires more energy per pound of body weight than a large adult cat. This is because in relation to its body volume, the smaller animal has more skin surface through which the energy can be lost. This is the same principle that enables crushed ice to cool liquids more rapidly than an uncrushed ice cube.

The cat that is restricted to a small apartment or house will use much less energy than a cat that is accustomed to roaming the neighborhood and fields. The lactating queen may use up to three times as much energy while nursing a large litter as she would use during a nonlactating period. A young kitten uses up to three times as much energy per unit of body weight as does an adult cat that is not very active.

Water

Life cannot be sustained without the intake of water. It is the most important nutrient, as important as oxygen. The body's need for water exceeds its need for food. In the wild, cats do not usually drink more than once every twenty-four hours because they obtain most of their fluid intake from the carcasses of their prey, which are 70 percent water.

About one-half to two-thirds of the body is made up of water. It is the main component of body fluids, secretions, and excretions. Water is the principal component of cells, blood, and lymph. It carries food materials from one part of the body to the other. Water is the solvent for most products of digestion. It holds them in solution and permits them to pass through the intestinal wall into the bloodstream for use throughout the body. Water helps regulate body temperature, aids digestion, and helps sustain health with its effect on all body cells. Only with a generous intake of water can these bodily tasks be performed with any degree of competency. A light sprinkling of salt on your cat's food encourages ample drinking.

Having evolved in a desert environment, cats can tolerate dehydration with greater ease than many other mammals, including dogs and humans. Cats have the ability to concentrate their urine to a greater extent, the effect of which is to conserve water within the body. This adaptation has its limits, however. Long-term dehydration is life-threatening to cats as well as most other creatures. The tendency to concentrate their urine causes some cats to drink less water than they should. Some researchers believe this to be part of the cause of blockages that form in the urinary tract. It is vital that all cats have free access to fresh water at all times and be encouraged to drink it. Kittens require more water intake in proportion to their body weight than adult cats.

Water is obtained from drinking, moisture found in food, and moisture produced as a product of metabolism. It leaves the body in urine, feces, vomit, air that is breathed out, lactation, glandular secretions, and body injuries.

Protein

Protein supplies amino acids that are essential to a cat's growth and health. The most palatable and quality sources are fish, meat, vegetables, and eggs. The amino acid composition of a protein depends on the source of the protein and the food-processing methods.

Egg protein is probably the best-known source of balanced amino acids for cats. Other proteins from fish, meats, and vegetable sources, available in commercial rations, approximate the amino acids found in egg protein. Such better-quality proteins are well digested and absorbed. While moderate heat treatment in processing does not significantly reduce the value of the proteins, excessive heat may destroy some protein values.

Protein forms tissues such as hair and muscles and is combined with carbohydrates, fats, and minerals in the cat's body to form enzymes, hormones, various body fluids, and antibodies. A specific level of protein is needed by the cat to continue normal body processes. A ration containing, on an air-dry basis, 30 to 35 percent protein, about 8 percent fat, and 40 percent carbohydrates can meet the protein requirements for a normal cat. Although the minimum level found in good commercial diets is approximately 30 percent, the extra 5 percent is recommended since the added protein seems to help increase disease-fighting antibody production.

A large excess of protein can be tolerated fairly well by

the majority of healthy cats. Excess nitrogen is broken away from the protein or amino acid molecules and is eliminated through the urine. Most of the remaining excess protein is metabolized as energy in the body or may be converted and stored as fat. While this excess protein may not be harmful to young, healthy cats, it may be extremely harmful to cats with liver damage and may be harmful to older cats with impaired circulation. Cats with liver and kidney damage tend to accumulate excess nitrogen in the body, so it is dangerous to feed them an extremely high protein diet (too much meat).

The cat owner, if he or she decides to feed extra meat, fish, or other protein sources to the cat, should cook these foods before adding them to the bowl. Uncooked egg white, for example, contains an antibiotin enzyme that is harmful to the cat. Most fresh fish contain an antithiamine enzyme, which can cause a thiamin deficiency in the cat, resulting in anorexia (loss of appetite), paralysis, abnormal reflexes, convulsions, and a general breakdown of the nervous system. Cook all fish. Cook all eggs, especially the whites.

Carbohydrates

Carbohydrates include starch, sugars (plant and milk), fibers, gums, and other storage components. Most cat foods are largely composed of carbohydrates, which supply the most inexpensive source of energy. When properly prepared, carbohydrates are well utilized by normal cats.

Carbohydrates form glycogen, by which the body stores energy, chiefly in the liver. Excess carbohydrates are converted to fat. A deficiency of carbohydrates is rare because protein and fat are consumed for energy in their absence. Some sugars (carbohydrates) are efficiently used and tolerated by normal cats. Others, like lactose (milk sugar), can be harmful to cats. Many cats cannot synthesize adequate quantities of the enzyme lactase, required for digestion of the milk sugar. This is particularly true of older cats. When the lactase level is low and lactose is high, the lactose tends to ferment in the digestive tract and can produce diarrhea. This is why some cats tend to have diarrhea when given too much cow's milk. Young kittens fed too much cow's milk may suffer digestive upset for the same reason.

Carbohydrates are thought to be necessary to provide energy and to regulate water absorption in the lower digestive tract. The amount to feed depends on the amounts of other nutrients making up the diet, but the maximum carbohydrate content in the diet of an average cat should not exceed 65 percent (by dry weight).

Fat

Fat is a concentrated source of energy (or fuel) that provides over twice as much energy potential as carbohydrates or protein. It supplies essential fatty acids and carries vitamins A, D, E, and K. It is also what makes food taste good to a kitten, just as the most expensive and best-tasting steaks have a rich marbling of fat. Fats are required for the basic composition of cells. They are necessary for making fat-soluble vitamins perform their functions. Fat also imparts a protective covering under the skin and affords internal organs a cushion of insulation.

Fat comes in the form of oil or solid fat. Health care providers refer to all forms of fat interchangeably as *lipids*. Oil is fat that is liquid at room temperature. However, the term *fat* most often refers to the form that is solid at room temperature. Because of the unique nutritional requirements of cats, their diet should always include a greater fat content than other pet foods.

It is the higher fat and protein content of a premium kitten food that makes it superior, and more expensive. However, when a cat eats more calories than it expends, the body converts the excess nutrients to fat and stores them in the body. This is the principle cause of obesity in cats. Therefore, it is important to be sensible about how much food you serve your kitten. Fat that is stored in the body provides a quick source of energy when needed. A pound of fat contains 4,268 calories ready to go to work if called upon. The problem with fat cats is that their stored fat is seldom called upon and instead lies on top of the body and eventually does harm.

As a rule, kittens consume more calories per pound of body weight than adult cats. Show cats, pregnant cats, nursing cats, high-energy cats all require more calories than the average adult cat that sleeps most of the day. Consult a veterinarian about the nutritional requirements of your cat.

Vitamins

Vitamins play a dynamic role in body processes of cats. They take part in the release of energy from foods, promote normal growth of different kinds of tissue, and are essential to the proper functioning of nerves and muscles. They are required in extremely small quantities but are essential for life. Researchers have identified and analyzed more than a dozen major vitamins essential to the cat diet. They have broadly categorized them into two groups, depending on their solubility. One group includes the *fat-soluble* vitamins A, D, E, and K, and the other includes the *water-soluble* B-complex and C vitamins. The cat's body can synthesize some vitamins from within utilizing various food nutrients, while other vitamins must be present in the diet.

Fat-soluble vitamins tend to oxidize easily. This means that fats that are becoming rancid or that have been oxidized excessively may be devoid of these vitamins. This is why old or rancid fats or oils should not be fed to cats. Cats seem to have a much greater tendency to exhibit muscular disintegration than other animals as a result of eating rancid fats.

Fat-soluble vitamins (A, D, K, and E). When absorbed and combined with fat, these vitamins are in part stored with fat deposits in the body. When stored in excess, they can eventually become toxic.

Vitamin A is an antioxidant (a substance that protects cells from damage caused by oxidation) and is necessary for normal growth, reproduction, physical maintenance of tissues, hearing, and vision. It also helps keep the skin and inner linings of the body healthy and resistant to infection. It is present in foods of animal origin. Many vegetables and fruits, particularly the green and yellow ones, contain a substance called carotene that most animals can change into vitamin A. However, the cat seems to have an extremely poor ability to use carotene as a source of vitamin A. Cats can utilize vitamin A from chemical or animal sources efficiently. Liver is an outstanding source of vitamin A. Significant amounts exist in eggs, butter, whole milk, and cheese made with whole milk.

Vitamin D is important in building strong bones and teeth because it enables the feline body to use calcium and phosphorus. Vitamin D requirements are reportedly much lower for adult cats than for kittens, and there appears to be more danger of overdoing with vitamin D than of deficiencies. Few foods contain much vitamin D naturally. Milk with vitamin D added is a practical source if your cat is one who can tolerate it. Small amounts of vitamin D are present in egg yolk, butter, kidneys, fish oil, and liver. Larger amounts occur in sardines, salmon, herring, and tuna. Direct sunlight is another source.

Vitamin K supports the clotting factor within the blood. Under normal conditions it is synthezised in the intestinal tract of cats and other animals. During stress or certain medications it may not be produced in sufficient quantities for normal requirements. For this reason vitamin K (menadione bisulfite) is added to many commercial cat foods. Vitamin K is found in green vegetables and is also synthesized by bacteria in the intestine. Do not supplement this vitamin without veterinary advice.

Vitamin E, another important antioxidant, supports the immune system. Older cats require more vitamin E than younger ones. The major sources of this vitamin are unrefined soybean, cottonseed, and corn oils; wheat germ; whole grains; and nuts. It is also found in smaller quantities in green vegetables, beans, and eggs.

Water-soluble vitamins (B and C). These vitamins are absorbed from the intestine and not stored in the body. Because they are not stored, cat owners should replenish them frequently as part of the diet or possibly by supplementation. Consult a veterinarian.

Vitamin C (ascorbic acid) is normally synthesized from glucose, making supplementation unnecessary except in the case of severe infection or stress. This vitamin's capabilities are controversial among scientists and researchers. What all accept is that it creates collagen, a gelatinous material that helps hold the body's cells in place, as well as assisting in normal tooth and bone formation, and aids in healing wounds. Probably the most controversial questions about vitamin C concern its role in aiding the body's immune system. The controversy centers on the effectiveness of vitamin C as a therapy for the common cold, cancer, and other diseases. Vitamin C occurs naturally in citrus fruits, strawberries, cantaloupe, watermelon, tomatoes and tomato juice, broccoli, brussels sprouts, cabbage, cauliflower, green peppers, and some dark-green leafy vegetables such as collards, kale, mustard greens, spinach, and turnip greens, in addition to potatoes and sweet potatoes, especially when baked in the skin.

Vitamin B and B complex are water-soluble and not stored in the body. They can be given separately or combined in one convenient B complex pill.

Vitamin B$_1$ (thiamine) is required by cats in unusually high amounts. Thiamine helps convert glucose into energy or fat. When thiamine is reduced in the cat's body, its energy level is seriously diminished. Thiamine deficiencies in cats can produce appetite loss, vomiting, weight loss, dehydration, paralysis, prostration, abnormal reflexes, convulsions, and cardiac disorders. Extra carbohydrates, such as bread and potatoes, and extra exercise increase the cat's requirements for thiamine. The need for thiamine is decreased slightly when higher levels of fat are added; thus composition of the diet influences the vitamin requirement. Sources of thiamine include whole grains (especially wheat germ and rice bran and polishings), brewer's yeast, pork, milk, nuts, liver, peas, soybeans, and most other beans.

Vitamin B$_2$ (riboflavin) is one of three B vitamins (thiamine, riboflavin, and niacin) that play a central role in the release of energy from food. They also help promote proper functioning of nerves, normal appetite, good digestion, and healthy skin. Riboflavin is important in many body processes, especially those involving skin, eyes, and the linings of the mouth and digestive tract. The body's demand for riboflavin increases in abnormal situations, for instance lactation or infections during the growth period.

Vitamin B₃ (niacin) is necessary for good health, growth, and reproduction. It supports the digestive system, nervous system, and the conversion of food to energy. Niacin also promotes healthy skin. It must be provided by supplement unless it is listed in the ingredients of the commercial cat food you use. This vital B vitamin is contained in dairy products, poultry, fish, lean meats, nuts, and eggs. It is also found in brewer's yeast, wheat germ, whole grains, liver, and kidney.

Vitamin B₅ (pantothenic acid) is an important support for cell replacement and growth. Excellent pantothenic acid sources are brewer's yeast, liver, kidney, heart, wheat germ, and whole grains.

Vitamin B₆ (pyridoxine) is one of several co-enzymes that help metabolize amino acids. It also helps make possible the utilization of carbohydrates in the body and is essential to facilitate the various aspects of metabolism. The best sources of pyridoxine are meat, egg yolks, liver, whole grains, brewer's yeast, heart, and blackstrap molasses.

Vitamin B₁₂ (cobalamin) is essential for the function of all cells in the body, but especially for bone marrow, production of red blood cells, the central nervous system, and the intestinal tract. It is essential for the prevention and cure of some types of anemia and is necessary for the development of young kittens. The synthesis of vitamin B₁₂ by intestinal bacteria combined with the B₁₂ found in the ingredients used to make cat foods helps ensure that a deficiency will not occur. Vitamin B₁₂ is found in whole grains, meat, fish, oysters, clams, yeast, and liver.

Biotin (part of the vitamin B complex group) is produced by intestinal synthesis in normal cats. It is essential

for the metabolism of all nutritional elements including carbohydrates, protein, and fat. This nutrient is inactivated by
uncooked egg whites, which is why raw eggs are not recommended for cats. Biotin is found in many foods including
cooked egg yolk, milk, liver, and yeast.

Choline (part of the vitamin B complex group) is important for the metabolizing of fats and in many biochemical reactions. It is also essential for normal liver function. Choline
is obtained from liver, kidney, various meats, wheat germ,
brewer's yeast, vegetables, and egg yolk.

Minerals

Minerals are necessary in the feline diet and enter practically
every phase of body activity. Cats would not live very long
on a diet devoid of minerals. Minerals maintain the acid-
base balance and tissue condition within the body and help
regulate most body activities.

Because of their interrelationships, minerals should always be considered as a group and never as separate entities.
Their requirements and proper ratio are affected by a
change in any one. If large doses of calcium are given im-
properly, for example, a diet that is otherwise adequate in all
trace minerals may become deficient in some.

Minerals are essential for preserving acid-base balance,
tissue structure, and fluid movement within the body, as well
as constituting essential components of various enzyme systems. Some minerals, although important for maintaining
good health, may be harmful when larger-than-necessary
amounts are given. Such is the case with the calcium-phosphorus ratio. These two minerals must always be discussed
together because of the interrelationship between the two.
When a deficiency or an imbalance between them occurs,
poor bone growth or maintenance results. Calcium is the

most abundant mineral element in the body. Most of the body's calcium is found in bones and teeth. Combined with phosphorus in the proper ratio, it is largely responsible for the hardness of these structures.

The small amount of calcium in other body tissues and fluids aids in the proper functioning of the heart, muscles, and nerves and helps the blood coagulate during bleeding. Bone formation seems to be optimal when the levels of calcium and phosphorus are adequate and when such associated nutrients as magnesium, vitamin D, choline, fluorine, and manganese are present in adequate and balanced quantities. A large excess of calcium can paradoxically produce a calcium deficiency.

The proper ratio of minerals is extremely important, but there is none more critical than the calcium-phosphorus ratio. The ratio should remain at *approximately* one part calcium to one part phosphorus. Some foods have a very poor calcium-phosphorus balance. Lean meat contains approximately 0.1 percent calcium and 0.18 percent phosphorus, for a ratio of almost one to two. If a cat owner wants to add lean meat to the cat's diet, the meat should be supplemented with a good commercial diet that can contribute the needed calcium. Calcium or calcium-and-phosphorus supplements should be added to a cat's ration only in carefully controlled quantities. It is important to consult your veterinarian before supplementing your cat's diet, especially with a calcium-phosphorus supplement.

Other minerals that have been established as essential to good feline health are magnesium, potassium, sodium and chloride, iron and copper, iodine, zinc, manganese, cobalt, and selenium.

What, When, and How Much to Feed Kittens

Kittens may double or triple their birth weight during the first three weeks of life, which is part of a rapid growth phase that lasts until twenty-one weeks of age. After that, growth slows down but does not stop until approximately twelve months. At six months of age, a kitten may look full grown, but its internal organs, muscles, teeth, and hair coat continue to develop until twelve months of age, and much later in some cats. Consequently, cats require more nutrition per pound of body weight in their first year than they do thereafter. This accelerated nutritional need ends once the cat has reached his adult stage. Owners must be guided by the performance of the diet rather than by the quantity of food eaten, because some foods have a higher concentration of nutrients than others, even though they may have less bulk. Steady growth, good health, a high energy level, a glossy coat, and a thin layer of fat beneath the skin indicate good nutritional performance. The rate of weight gain depends on the individual cat, its temperament, environmental considerations (including weather), and its level of activity. Weigh the cat once a week and maintain a record of its rate of weight gain. This will indicate whether the diet is sufficient. Ideally, you should consult a veterinarian about how much to feed your kitten. Most premium kitten foods provide feeding guidelines on their label.

From birth to weaning, which means from day one to day twenty-eight (or thereabouts), mother's milk is the primary source of nourishment. This is adequate if the mother cat (the queen) has an ample milk supply for the entire litter. Important antibodies are present in her milk for the first twenty-four to thirty-six hours. Veterinarians call this substance *colostrum*. In addition to providing immunities, it also supplies essential quantities of protein, vitamins, and various nutrients necessary for the newborn kittens. It is essential that the kittens receive colostrum as soon as possible after being born. If the kittens become orphans or are rejected by the mother for any reason, it is imperative to supply nourishment as quickly as possible if they are to survive. There are several high-quality breast milk replacement products available for orphaned newborn kittens, all of which a veterinarian can suggest. It is important to understand that feline breast milk has a higher percentage of protein and fat than cow's milk. For that reason, cow's milk does not meet the nutritional requirements of kittens, although as a *temporary* substitute it's better than nothing.

Follow your veterinarian's directions for feeding the breast milk replacement—your vet will provide quantities and feeding times—or simply follow the direction on the label of the product. Most newborn kittens require four or five feedings a day and receive fewer than two teaspoons per feeding. These commercial products often come with nipples and bottles to help you feed the kitten properly.

If you bottle-feed an orphaned kitten, bear in mind that he must have direct stimulation to help him digest his food for the first two weeks of his life. You will have to burp the little cat by gently patting his back and then help him to urinate and defecate by rubbing him on the belly. Normally, the mother cat would do this with her tongue.

By four weeks of age, the kitten is ready to be weaned away from a milk-only diet with the gradual introduction of whole food. For two or three weeks, you can introduce a commercially prepared cereal product for weaning kittens. Mix it with tepid whole or evaporated milk and feed a small quantity four times a day between nursing sessions with the mother or scheduled milk replacement feedings. An alternative is to offer commercial kitten food that you have moistened with the milk replacer formula. In the sixth week, introduce small quantities of cooked, scraped meat or gently cooked mild fish or white-meat chicken. You may also offer commercial kitten food that has been slightly moistened with water or broth.

How much to feed a kitten. The growth rate of kittens accelerates during the first twenty-one weeks. Some cats, however, do not reach full maturity for fifteen to eighteen months. An eight-week-old kitten, fully weaned, requires four meals a day, consisting of approximately one ounce of food per meal. Provide a minimum of four to five ounces of food per day for each kitten. Vary the diet from meal to meal with dry food formulated for kittens, cooked egg yolk, small quantities of whole milk (provided it does not cause indigestion), strained meats (baby food), cooked fish, cooked chicken breast, or a small quantity of raw or cooked liver.

By five months of age, provide your kitten with no less than six ounces of food daily and switch from four to three meals a day. Three feedings a day are desirable for kittens up to eight months of age.

Many cats, when allowed, will become addicted to or insist on one or two foods only. This can be a problem if the food is not complete and balanced or if, for some medical reason, you must change your cat's diet. For these and other reasons, a variety of food should be provided to your cat for his entire life. Try to avoid food addictions or fixation to any one type or brand. Do not humanize your cat's diet in order to make it more palatable. Human nutritional needs and cat needs are different, although cats will eat human food because of the attention that goes along with it or because they find some of it palatable. Bear in mind that every cat is different and only the most general rules apply to all. To some extent, you should follow the dictates of your own kitten to determine food quantities, feeding schedules, and types of food offered. Avoid getting into a battle of the wills with your kitten. You will lose, and a standoff can lead to malnutrition. And remember to make clean, fresh water available at all times.

How much to feed an adult cat. Feed an active, ten-pound adult male cat (unneutered) a total of six to twelve ounces of regular canned food; eight to eleven ounces of canned gourmet food; from two to five ounces of soft-moist food; or from three to four ounces of premium, complete, and balanced dry food.

Adult cats require approximately thirty-six calories of food for every pound of body weight. This ratio may vary depending on your cat's activity level, other pets in the household, environmental influences such as cold or hot weather, lactation, or the need to recover from surgery. You can best maintain the health of an adult cat with two meals a day, spaced between eight and ten hours apart. Remember, the proper amount of food is the amount that allows the cat to maintain its ideal body weight on a consistent basis, without radical gain or loss.

One of the biggest mistakes some pet owners make is feeding commercial dog food to a cat. Cats need significantly more protein and fat in their diet than dogs. The feline body also requires more B complex vitamins than dogs. Cats easily absorb iron from meat, while dogs do not.

Vitamin supplements. This subject is among the more controversial matters pertaining to feeding cats and kittens. Manufacturers of premium pet food tell us that supplements are not necessary because they have formulated vitamins and minerals into their products. Vitamin and mineral manufacturers claim that supplements are necessary because there is no way of knowing if the individual cat's needs are being met by the food or if the cat is eating enough to satisfy its requirements.

Veterinarians are divided on this subject, and the advice given depends on the vet's orientation, from holistic to traditional and everything in between. Cats cannot convert some of the amino acids of protein into needed vitamins (specifically, tryptophan into niacin). The cat's body chemistry cannot synthesize from within most vitamins and in some cases, such as vitamin C, cannot store what it isn't using. For this reason, it is a good idea to add supplements to your kitten's diet. However, *do not go overboard with supplements.* Some people believe that if one amount is healthy for the animal, then ten times that amount must be better. This is absolutely untrue and unsafe. Oversupplementing can be toxic and create a condition known as *hypervitaminosis*, which is more common than vitamin deficiency, *hypovitaminosis*. Consult a veterinarian for advice on supplements for your kitten.

Home-cooked meals for cats. If you are planning on cooking for your kitten, it is not enough to scrape some food off your plate or to prepare a menu that you know the kitten likes. Just because a kitten will eat whatever you put on its plate doesn't mean he is getting a diet that provides enough for growth and health maintenance, meeting his nutritional requirements.

To do it properly, you will need a chart concerning the

recommended nutrient allowances for kittens and cats, a chart indicating the ideal rations for kittens and cats, and a chart showing the daily food requirements of kittens and cats. You may be able to obtain such charts from a pet food manufacturer or from a government agency.

Next you must obtain a lengthy chart showing the nutritional values of the basic foods you will cook for your kitten, breaking them down into their percentages of protein, carbohydrates, fats, vitamins, and minerals. Once you know the nutritional value of human foods, match them up against the nutritional requirements charts and create a sensible menu based on your kitten's nutritional requirements. Here too the keynote is variety. It is especially important to add vitamin and mineral supplements with home-cooked meals for kittens. All this work is necessary to provide a proper home-cooked feeding regimen for a kitten. A complete and balanced commercially manufactured premium kitten food sounds like a better idea.

If you are going to introduce human foods to your cat's diet, here are some useful tips. All fish must be cooked before feeding. Most cats like fish, but it can be addictive to the exclusion of all other forms of protein. Be sensible about the quantity given and the frequency with which it is fed. Excessive amounts of canned or fresh fish can bring about an ailment known as *steatitis* (body fat inflammation), which can be fatal. Milk is not essential in your adult cat's diet. Some cats will drink milk, but most cannot digest it properly because of a lack of necessary enzymes. Diarrhea is usually the result. Pregnant or lactating queens do need an added source of calcium. Good alternative calcium sources are cheese, yogurt, canned salmon, cottage cheese, collard greens, kale, and turnip greens. Tomato juice is beneficial for acidifying the urine in cats with a predisposition for urinary disease. Cooked vegetables offer some vitamins and minerals and are desirable if the cat likes them. A teaspoon of animal fat or butter once a day is beneficial. Do not feed your cat an exclusive diet of liver or other organ meats (raw or cooked) or even large amounts on a random basis. They provide an excess of vitamin A, which adversely affects the bone structure.

Commercial Cat Food

Dry, cereal type. Dry cat food consists of grains or cereals mixed with combinations of meat, fish, and/or dairy products. The premium brands have added vitamins and minerals, balanced to meet the nutritional requirements of cats.

Dry cat food is the most economical form of commercial food for cats. Because of the high density of the food, the cat owner is not purchasing large amounts of water. The moisture content of dry food is 10 percent. Canned foods contain between 70 and 76 percent moisture, making it necessary to feed a cat larger portions in order to maintain adequate nutrition. Cost therefore becomes a consideration. Many cats love to crunch their food, and one of the easiest ways of feeding is to select a top-quality dry food product and put it in a bowl in a quiet, convenient place, allowing your cat to eat whenever he is hungry.

Soft-moist cat food. This form of commercial cat food comes in various colors and is soft to the touch, yet it does not require refrigeration. It is often made to resemble hamburger, stew meat, or meat granules. Cats tend to be attracted to the look, smell, and taste of it. It is made with many protein sources; it may feature only one as the overall flavoring, such as beef or tuna, or may offer flavor mixtures. More expensive than dry food, it is formulated to provide complete nutrition.

Canned cat food. Canned cat food is by far the most popular form of food used to feed house cats. The ingredients consist of some form of protein (most often fish or poultry), along with various grains and vitamins and mineral supplements. These are cooked in the can and preserved through the traditional canning process. In addition to its great taste appeal, canned food provides a significant quantity of water for all cats, because they usually do not drink as much as they should. Canned cat food contains almost 75 percent moisture and helps maintain your cat's water balance.

Canned "gourmet" cat food. Of the canned cat foods, these are the most expensive and, interestingly, the most popular. They appeal to our human desire to indulge our pets. They come in such flavors as kidney, liver, chicken, shrimp, tuna, beef, and many combinations of these ingredients. This form of commercial food is best when used as part of an overall feeding program. Do not feed this type exclusively.

Commercial cat food for special needs. These products are mostly formulated for feeding sick or obese cats. Most of the cat food you buy at a supermarket or feed store is intended for normal kittens and average adult cats. While some of those foods are of higher quality than others, their intended use is still the same, which is to nourish a typically healthy pet.

However, when your cat is sick or overweight, you must change his regular diet to conform with a veterinarian's therapy. A convenient alternative to preparing special formulas at home is a commercially prepared canned or dry food that is obtained from your veterinarian. Although these prescribed diets are available in a maintenance formula, they are also formulated specifically for cats suffering with diabetes, colitis, obesity, food allergies, heart conditions, kidney disorders, liver disorders, and many other illnesses. Such food can only be obtained from a licensed veterinarian.

Cats, like humans, need varied types and amounts of food at different times in their lives. Obviously a kitten eats differently than an adult cat. This chapter's guidelines to feline nutrition will help you provide your kitten with optimal nutrition throughout his life. The elements of this chapter can be useful throughout the life of your cat.

Little angels need to be trained.

NINE

TRAINING KITTENS

Kittens are little angels when they cuddle in your arms but become big-time mischief makers when you fall asleep or leave them alone. Expect it. They pounce on lamp cords and sometimes pull the lamps off the table. They knock books off shelves or smash breakables to the ground. They can open cabinet doors and get into the cat food or the Brillo. A clothes closet can be a test of feline courage, a tempting adventure as they gnaw on your most expensive pumps. Let's not even discuss their plucking the satin stripes on the upholstery with their sharp nails as though they were banjo strings.

The compulsion to pounce on your moving ankles is also a normal part of kitten growth and development. Shoelaces become a mortal enemy and anything that rolls along the floor is a make-believe meal trying to escape. Kittens will always rise to that challenge, unless of course there is carpet fringe that requires their attention. These activities are dramatized learning experiences, like a porcelain vase deliberately pushed off the shelf to see if it will run or fight back.

The noise of its crash to the floor is always an interesting surprise to little cats, who will either run from it or stare down with pride and curiosity at the broken pieces. When kittens play, they are instinctively learning how to hunt or fight. It is feline theater—rehearsals for the day when events are no longer play. And then there is always the possibility of using a bed spread for a place to urinate or staring blankly at you when you call. For all of these reasons, and more, you may find the idea of training your cat quite attractive.

The Truth About Cat Training

Cats are very different from dogs because they can get much of what they need on their own without intricate social interactions. They do not express their social behavior in the same way as dogs. At the root of social behavior in most animals is the instinct to survive, but the terms of survival are unique to any given species. In the natural state cats (except for lions) do not usually live in social groups like dogs. As nongroup animals, they have their own unique approach to the survival aspects of territory, food, and mating. Their acceptance of the human environment can be attributed to their many, many generations of domesticity, which means they have been nurtured into a state of perpetual adolescence and partial dependency. Human parental expressions of love and affection are irresistible. Although adult cats are not helpless and totally dependent, the lusty fragrance of a freshly opened bag of cat food represents an easier life than hunting for something to eat in the tall grass. Besides, in nature, there is always something eager to make a meal of *you*. The good pet life does offer many comforts and benefits.

Humans can train dogs to obey spoken commands and hand signals. Dogs live in groups known as packs and are motivated to learn and then obey your commands by their instinct to secure a place in your family (which is a substitute dog pack). They will work for human acceptance and affection by responding appropriately to corrections and rewards. Training kittens (and adult cats) is not remotely like training dogs.

Training a cat is a limited pursuit and you cannot have the same expectations that you would of dogs. In fact, most people believe you cannot train cats at all, which is not entirely true. Training a kitten is special, even though it can be like putting toothpaste back in the tube. It is hard to do unless you know how to induce a cat to behave within the boundaries of its natural inclinations, which is to do as it pleases. You certainly cannot frighten or punish a kitten into obeying you. It just doesn't work. However, a cat will do anything you ask of it, as long as there is something in it for him, or he feels like doing it.

As everyone knows, kittens are always getting into trouble. It is their birthright. It has to do with curiosity, growing up, and learning how to be a cat. Nevertheless, mischievous or destructive behavior must be changed, controlled, or at least supervised. You must wean kittens away from unacceptable behavior, as well teaching them a few basic things; to use the litter pan, to come to you when you call, and to stop doing something bad because you say so. This is where channeling natural feline behavior becomes important. You will need to introduce these things differently from the way you would with an adult cat. Experienced cat people think of it as behavior management, but you can call it cat training if you like.

What Is Cat Training, Anyway?

Although there are several approaches to cat training, the most effective is to take advantage of feline natural behavior such as running, playing, jumping, or hunting by teaching the kitten to do these things at your command, using food treats as a reward. Bear in mind that barking out orders with a demanding tone of voice does nothing but frighten a kitten and has no positive effect. With a kitten, you should be pleasantly firm and entice him with your voice and body language, making sweet requests of your so-called commands. (Begging and pleading do not count.) Cat training is based on knowing the predictable behavior patterns and minor vices of your cat and rechanneling his reaction to a verbal demand from you. By knowing what pleases your cat, you can reinforce his responses to your "commands" with treats and with affection and playful attention. Some call it bribery, but think of it as creating desirable patterns of behavior with the use of positive reinforcement.

Training kittens is especially difficult because they are easily distracted and so full of hiss and vinegar. They can be single-minded or pretend to be deaf to whatever you say. However, if you smear a bit of butter on their toes, you can refocus their attention; a commercial cat snack will capture their interest; offer freshly cooked hamburger, and they'll follow you into the jaws of hell. On the other hand, kittens can be easy to train because everything that happens is a new experience and curiosity can make them eager students, especially if there is a delectable payment for their efforts.

Contrary to popular belief, you must train kittens to some degree if they are going to live with you. For example, they need to learn their name so that you can get their attention easily. You must teach them to use the litter pan for toileting and no other place. You must teach them *not* to destroy furniture and human flesh with their nails. Only you can get across the idea that it is bad to climb the curtains like a tree. You can teach them to come to you when you call, to walk with you on a leash (if it's practical), to sit when you tell them, and most important of all, to stop what they're doing when you say *no!* These are the basics and very doable. Tricks such as dancing on their hind legs or sitting in a wagon dressed in a satin-and-sequin cape wearing sunglasses are not necessary. Such demands are also disrespectful, undignified, and lacking in appreciation for a cat's natural attractiveness. As your kitten grows into an adult, it is far more important to teach him to come to you when you call if you need to groom him or get him into his travel carrier. That is a more positive use of training.

Strictly speaking, the word *training* refers to behavior modification where you condition an animal to respond to something that triggers specific actions, especially if the desired response is contrary to his species' typical behavior. *Behavior management* is a more accurate term when referring to cats. Teaching a kitten to use the litter pan merely requires showing him where it is and giving one initial lesson on how to use it. He will take it from there. It doesn't even require a food treat. Most other feline training involves the redirection of normal behavior to where you want it by offering a food treat or some form of affection or play. In other words, if something good happens (a food treat) when he listens to you, then the kitten will learn to go along with what you want once a pattern of behavior is established by constant repetition. It's very Pavlovian (based on the research of Ivan Pavlov, 1904 Nobel Laureate, and the American psychologist B. F. Skinner from his mid-twentieth-century research at Harvard University). Call the cat to you, offer a reward, and ring a bell (or snap a clicker), or say something nice immediately following the reward. That's cat training.

Basic Training for Kittens

Many cat breeders and experienced cat owners know that the most important factor in a kitten's ability to live happily with humans and to be reasonably trained is its opportunity to be *socialized* by the first humans in its life. This simply means that a human being handles and cuddles a kitten many times a day in the earliest weeks of its life. Although this prescription may sound simple and obvious, it is amazing how many kittens never get this form of attention in the first four or five weeks of their lives, when it is most crucial, and then grow up to be distant with humans and suspicious and frightened of anything not familiar. As adults, such cats can become difficult to manage. For training purposes, the ideal situation is to have the kitten imprint on you as early as possible. The best results occur when you start talking to a kitten around the fourth day of life, even before his eyes have opened. If you talk to him and caress him frequently, imprinting on you will take place. *Imprinting* is a learning process limited to a specific developmental period that leads to an extremely rapid conditioning. If the animal focuses on the imprinting object—in this case, you—during the very early or sensitive period, the animal will always prefer the imprinted object. The most heartwarming example of imprinting is the way newly hatched ducklings follow their mother in a single line as she waddles toward the pond. If the imprinting object were a dog, the ducklings would follow him and consider him to be mama.

In addition to socialization, objects such as toys, spools, balls, and other objects of play to stimulate mental and physical activity should be available to a kitten. If these elements are introduced early in a kitten's life, he will be a much friendlier cat and more adaptive to learning from you. Of course, staying with the original litter and with the mother cat is more than simply fun; it is another means of learning and socializing. Kittens should stay with their littermates and their mothers at least until they are weaned to solid food and even longer if possible, because there are aspects of feline education that only a mother cat can teach, including hunting skills. Rarely will a pedigreed cat breeder release a precious kitten before three months of age, and many will wait longer than that. However, loving human contact is essential as early as possible. A socialized cat will respond to training more enthusiastically, but it is never too late to socialize a cat, even an older cat, to some degree. (Socializing a feral or free-roaming cat can be a lot harder—impossible in some cases.)

Part of socializing is teaching your kitten his name. This is actually an important aspect of cat training. The minute you bring your kitten into your home, you must begin to develop a relationship with him and allow him to get to know you. You can accomplish this by showering the little cat with attention and affection, which happens automatically anyway.

Hold the kitten close to you, talk to him in soft, sometimes loving, sometimes playful tones. Never, never be harsh. Never frighten your kitten. Talk to him when you feed him, when you carry him around, when you play. Be a well-defined, gentle presence so that he looks to you for protection, food, and guidance. In a sense, you must be the top cat. If you pay close attention to a kitten, you may notice that he will glance your way just before he gets into trouble. When human toddlers do this, they are either daring you to stop them or hoping you will save them from their own behavior. If you're watching your kitten, you have an opportunity to stop him. Your very presence can be commanding without your saying a word. However, gentleness is important above all. A kitten's basic training has as much to do with human behavior as it does with feline behavior. You must always give your cat some important part of your daily attention. Feed him. Play with him. Talk to him. Touch him. It's very basic.

A Short Course in Kitten Training

Training a cat requires using his predictable behavior patterns and minor vices. By knowing what pleases him, you can develop his responses to your commands through food, affection, and inducements to play.

Teaching the Use of the Litter Pan

WHAT IT'S ALL ABOUT

There is more to a kitten's pee and poop than nutrition, digestion, and elimination of body waste. A cat's scent is his signature. He uses his body waste as scent posts for the purpose of claiming territory, declaring his dominance, and communicating with other cats.

Females in heat and males looking for females in heat mark off areas with their urine to attract each other. In this situation the urine contains glandular secretions that give it an odor with sexual meanings.

Body waste is also connected to health functions. Frequency of elimination and the appearance of feces and urine often indicate your cat's state of health. The first place for a veterinarian to look for parasites is in the feces. All of these factors may be involved in your cat's litter pan orientation. Therefore, when your cat suddenly stops using the litter pan, it may not be a simple matter of training or spite or anything concerning discipline. A sick or emotionally upset cat will have such failures. Solving the underlying problem is the only way to get the kitten back to using the proper toilet.

In the first two weeks of his life a kitten has no physical ability to eliminate on his own. Elimination is accomplished with the help of the mother, who simply licks the underbelly, thus stimulating urination and defecation. She ingests the body waste from the kitten so that no detectable odor comes from the nest. This natural response promotes survival because it prevents predators from locating the litter by its scent. Similarly, her own body waste is eliminated away from the nest and buried. It is for this reason and this reason exclusively that cats instinctively bury their body waste. For the cat owner this is a blessing, since a cat's natural instinct to keep his nest clean makes him the best of pets.

After the first three weeks of a newborn kitten's life, his eyes open, hearing develops, and just about all physical functions begin to work without outside stimulation. He becomes less helpless. The kitten begins to crawl and eventually gets himself outside the nest for a look at his new world. It is extraordinary that the youngster has already learned not to eliminate in his own nest. His mother is very strict about this and does not permit it. At this early age many kittens have already begun to travel a relatively far distance from the nest in order to relieve themselves and make infantile digging and burying gestures. All of this behavior works to the advantage of humans who wish to live with cats as companions and members of their family. Assuming a kitten has been with his mother and littermates for at least twelve weeks, litter pan orientation is an easy and quick process. Some kittens have been known to use the litter pan properly immediately after leaving their mother and former home.

For all of the same reasons previously described, few kittens or adult cats will use an unclean litter pan. If you do not scoop out the solid waste material from a litter pan at least once a day, and if you do not change the litter material at least once a week and wash the pan, your kitten will not use it. You can well imagine what happens next. The more frequently you clean the litter pan, the happier everyone will be, especially your kitten.

PROCEDURE

Step 1. Set up a litter pan before your kitten comes home. (See Chapter 4, "What to Buy for Your Kitten.") This is the most important item to have in your house for the exclusive use of your newest family member. Coming home with a new kitten is an exciting event for everyone, especially the kitten, so take a moment to first sit down with the little cat on your lap and let him calm down. The objective is to make him feel safe and protected.

Step 2. When things settle down, quietly walk to the litter pan while holding the kitten. Close the bathroom door and place him in the center of the pan, taking hold of his front paws. Gently push them deep into the contents of the pan and scrape them back and forth, simulating a scratching motion. In most situations, the kitten's instinct to eliminate will take over; although he may not eliminate each time. Do not force the issue. Allow the kitten to hop out of the pan if that is what he wants to do. Wherever the litter pan is placed (usually in the bathroom), be sure the kitten cannot run out. Wait a minute or two and then repeat the procedure. Depending on many things, the kitten will eventually give you the desired results. He should eliminate and then scratch the litter material to cover it up. *Voilà!* Once he uses the litter pan properly, give him a treat and a compliment. The kitten is guaranteed to use the litter pan as his toilet every time he needs it. It is hard to believe, but it is that easy. Of course, a treat is unnecessary once a behavior pattern has been established.

Step 3. Until you are absolutely sure the kitten understands all this, never give him the run of the house unless you are right there with him, ready to prevent a mistake. If he sniffs one spot constantly, scratches the floor, and then squats, scoop him up in your arms and carry him to the litter pan quickly, close the door behind you and repeat the front-paw scratching procedure. Afterwards, give him a food treat and tell him how smart and wonderful he is.

Confinement is a very important aspect of this teaching technique. Keep the kitten in the room with the litter box and nowhere else unless he is constantly supervised. Place a dish of water with him, and perhaps a toy or two. Young kittens need a little time to learn to find the room with the litter pan in it. Even a grown cat may decide to place a scent signal on the far wall of a new dining room simply because his behavior hasn't been patterned for use of the litter pan yet. Also, kittens may not be able to control their small bladders while on the way to the room with the litter box. Very few cats will deliberately soil their living space if they can help it. They are too fastidious.

Confining the kitten to one room helps him to pattern his behavior in the correct way by making the litter box more immediately available than any other place in the home. Once a cat soils outside the pan, he will constantly be attracted to the spot because of the odor. *Do not allow this to develop into a pattern, because it will be extremely difficult to change.* When a cat makes a mistake, it is important to clean it up and destroy the scent of urine as fast as you can. There are many products in pet supply stores designed to eradicate urine stains and odors. Remember, the odor (imperceptible to humans) is the most important signal that you need to eradicate.

Do not neglect or reject the idea of temporary confinement. Even a cat that has always used a litter pan should be confined when not supervised at least for the first twenty-four hours after moving into a new home. Continue to confine your kitten until you are certain he knows what to do and where to do it. Learning will probably happen with the first few uses of the litter pan. It shouldn't take more than two days, if that long. And that should end the necessity for confinement.

Name It and It's Yours

For a kitten, knowing its name is more than a cute trick. A kitten that has learned its name can be a lot easier to manage than one that doesn't. The next part of the training regimen is teaching your cat to respond to its name.

Cats are much smarter than most people think. Once a cat knows his name, he understands that it pertains to him exclusively and he will respond to it positively, providing it is to his advantage to do so.

Step 1. If you have not yet named your kitten, pick a name that is short and sweet, just one or two syllables, so the cat can more easily identify with it. If you name him something like SpongeBob SquarePants, you are going to draw a blank when you call to him. And try to keep the name positive-sounding so that it makes you feel good to call him. A name with a negative connotation or association can create a less-than-happy feeling whenever you or anyone else says it. Try to avoid such names as Dummy or Barfie or Fang. Stay away from sarcasm (*Dog*), social or political commentary (*Bushy*), and negative humor (*Martha Stewart*). These are provocative names with meanings far too weighty for a kitten. Because cats are lovable, beautiful, graceful, and regal animals, their names should reflect these qualities, giving everyone a good feeling. Magazine advertisements, literary characters, references in poetry, and admired celebrities are all good sources for cat names.

Your kitten will quickly learn to respond to his name if you have established a friendship between you. This involves a relationship based on trust, security, and affection. Without it, nothing will work.

Step 2. A kitten learns his own name by hearing it repeated frequently and associating it with something pleasant. Once you have given him a name, you must never use it in vain. Never say the cat's name in anger or as part of a punishment or as part of a scolding. You should only use your kitten's name in a pleasant context and in a happy, upbeat tone of voice. If the association is negative, no cat—or anyone else for that matter—will come running to your call.

Step 3. When teaching the cat his name, dole out a food

reward every time you say it and praise him lavishly as you do. Use the kitten's name frequently and at every opportunity. Call him at every opportune moment. Call him by name to dinner. When you give him a hug, say his name as you do it. When you feed him, say his name.

Coming When Called

Once you teach your kitten his name, you have practically trained him to come when you call him. However, bear in mind that you can never get a cat to obey because he wants to please you or is afraid of you. You can count on a frightened cat to run away. It is only on the simplest level that cats accept the dominant/subordinate idea at all, and chances are he thinks he is dominant over you anyway, so forget it.

Like their undomesticated cousins, house cats are always in search of food because they cannot get it into their dear heads that the electric can opener whirls on a regular basis. Your little cat is, in a sense, constantly on the hunt. He'll do almost anything for food. He might even go along with a command if there's something in it for him. If you're thinking about training a cat, especially a kitten, you might want to take advantage of his tendency to be hungry. When teaching your kitten something new, feed him his normal diet necessary to maintain him in a healthy condition. However, for training purposes feed your kitten slightly less food than usual so that he'll work for more food. You can take up the slack after the training session. A good alternative to this is to conduct training sessions shortly before the kitten's mealtime. Find a food reward that your kitten loves and will work for. Bits of cooked liver are quite effective. Cats work better when they are just a bit hungry. When a cat is full, all he wants to do is curl up and sleep and hang out the Do Not Disturb sign.

Step 1. Feed your kitten a tiny bit of food treat and say his name. Repeat this four or five times, always saying his name before handing over the treat. Rub his head each time and say something pleasant and enthusiastic such as, "Marvin is *such* a good cat!".

Step 2. Place the kitten in one end of the room and walk to the other. Call her by name and add the word "come": "Lu-lu, come." Don't forget to say it pleasantly and with enthusiasm. Make it a treat just to be called. Chances are your kitten will come running because she has just had demonstrated for her that there is a food treat waiting for her. When she gets to you, give her the treat and once again say, "Lu-lu is such a good cat." Repeat this exercise five or six times and then end the session.

Step 3. Repeat step 2 thirty minutes later. Give your kitten two sessions a day, spaced thirty minutes apart, for the rest of the week.

Step 4. At the next session on the following week, place the kitten in one end of the room and walk to the other. Call him by name and add the word "come." At the same time use a hand signal. Starting with your right arm hanging at your side, swing it upward and around as though beckoning so that you touch your left shoulder, then gently return to your original position. As you execute the hand signal, hold out your left hand with the food reward sitting on the flat of your palm. Bend forward slightly so that the kitten can lick the reward off your hand. Walk to the opposite end of the room and repeat the procedure. Do this five times if the cat performs well and ten times if he does not. Remember to call the kitten by name: "Marvin, come." Once again, work the kitten in two sessions, spaced apart, each day, and repeat for three days in a row. By this time your kitten should be coming to you whenever you call him. Once he has learned, call him by name at least once a day. Although you do not have to offer a food treat every time, it doesn't hurt to reinforce the procedure once in a while with a food tidbit as a reward.

Taking a Walk

Not everyone feels it is necessary to teach a cat to take a walk on a leash. It is an uncommon sight, to be sure. Almost all serious cat people believe it is just too dangerous to allow a cat out of the house to roam freely on his own, especially a kitten. They are absolutely right about that. An excellent compromise is to allow your cat the pleasure of the great outdoors by walking him as you would a puppy. Of course, it is best to walk where there are few distractions—such as noisy auto traffic, gawking kids or adults—and no dogs. Dogs can be frightening to any cat, especially a kitten.

Before setting out to teach this procedure, be certain that your kitten has a suitable temperament for it. A very shy, cowering cat, who would rather be home under the bed than anywhere else in the world, is a very poor candidate for walking on a leash outdoors. However, if your kitten is extremely curious, outgoing, and somewhat bold, then by all means give him the pleasure of your company by teaching him to take a walk with you.

Using the correct equipment for this is absolutely essential. Never teach a cat to walk with a leash and *collar*, which you would have to buckle far too tightly for it to remain around his neck. Instead use a cat harness, designed for this purpose. A well-fitted *figure-eight harness* is best, attached to a long, lightweight leash. The leash should be made of nylon just like the harness. A leather leash is usable if it is very narrow and lightweight and six feet long.

Step 1. Get the kitten used to wearing the harness and leash. Some cats will not mind at all, while others will resist with obstinate vigor and take a long time to make the adjustment. Start with the harness alone. Give it to the kitten as if it were a toy. Lay it at the cat's feet and allow him to sniff it, move it about, and even push it around. Once he is con-

The moment of truth: walking outdoors
while secured with a harness and leash.

vinced the harness is not dangerous, put it on. Allow the kitten to wear it for the better part of the day and then remove
it; repeat this for two days. It might even be a good idea to
place it in his bed so that he can claim it as his own territory.

Step 2. Tie a short strip of cloth or string to the harness
and put it on the kitten. Leave it on for most of the day. Be
sure to keep an eye on the kitten so he does not get himself
tangled around the strip. Take it off at the end of the day. Repeat this for two days in a row. Do not encourage the kitten
to play with the strip.

Step 3. Hook the actual leash to the harness instead of
the cloth strip or string and then place the harness on the cat.
This will, of course, feel different to the kitten. The greater
length and weight may be annoying. For the first day, hook
the leash to the harness for no more than thirty minutes at a
time, off and on throughout the day. Repeat this for two days.

Step 4. Repeat step 3, but this time pick up the leash in
your hand and walk along with the cat indoors only. It may
go well in the beginning if you are both walking in the same

direction. It may be a problem when you exert a bit of pressure on the leash and walk in another direction. The kitten will definitely balk and even dig in his paws. If he fights the leash, lies down, or strongly resists, bend down to the kitten's level, and speak softly and gently as you coax him to follow you. Have a food tidbit ready, and offer it as an inducement to walk to you. Once the kitten walks toward you, give him the reward, stand quickly, and begin to walk with him. Do not force the issue by pulling the kitten along, as this will only increase the cat's resistance. Cats never walk like an obedience-trained dog. Repeat this whole procedure for two days.

Step 5. The real test comes when you attempt to walk your kitten wearing a harness and leash, outside. When your kitten is exposed to the sidewalk, he is going to be frightened at first; he will want to run and hide or may just freeze in one spot. Hold the kitten in your arms for as long as necessary, even for the entire first couple of outings. Talk to him lovingly and reassuringly. Give him a food tidbit. Try to create a very pleasant association with this first outdoor experience. If the kitten has calmed down a bit in your arms, kneel, place him on the ground, using reassuring statements and food rewards. Be very patient and very sensitive to his fear. Eventually, a typical, healthy kitten will make an adjustment and walk as you walk. At the start, allow the cat to walk anywhere he wants, unless he heads for the street. Let him have his way. If the kitten walks anywhere when outdoors while hooked to the harness and leash, it is major progress; your being able to set the direction of the walk comes later and without force. Repeat all this for several days in a row and you will have turned the corner.

Whether he's fully trained or not, be prepared at all times to pick your kitten up if a stray dog or other potential threat appears, or you may find yourself serving as an impromptu tree climbed by a terrified kitten equipped with many razor-sharp claws.

Teaching "Jump," "Sit," "Stand," and "Down" as One Command

Teaching your kitten to jump onto a chair or counter top at your direction, then to sit, rise on his hind legs, and leap back to the floor sounds more difficult than it is. Like all so-called cat training, it simply requires channeling a cat's normal behavior. Here again the key is to reward the kitten with a food treat. When teaching these movements, be sure the kitten is just a bit hungry.

Step 1. Put the kitten through the paces described in "Coming When Called." Once he comes to you, give him a food reward, immediately followed by verbal praise.

Step 2. Kneel down slowly, keeping his attention on you by staring in his eyes. Say, "Sit," and gently push his hind section down into a sitting position, give him a food reward, and offer ·him lavish praise. Repeat this five times and then quit. Conduct another session one or two hours later, doing the whole thing over again. Repeat this each day until the kitten will sit on signal, without your having to push his rear end down.

Step 3. Get him to jump onto a chair or a counter top if it's not too high. While the cat is at one end of a room, set up a stool at the other end. In a friendly but firm voice say the cat's name, followed by "Come." Use the hand signal for coming when called. When the kitten gets to you, kneel down and give him a food treat. Praise him. Then say, "Sit." If he sits for you, give him another food treat; immediately praise him.

Step 4. Stand up and hold out a food reward with your hand halfway up the length of the stool. The cat will probably try to reach for it while still in a sitting position. Say his name and "Jump." If he starts to get poised as if he is going to jump, place the hand holding the food reward slightly above the height of the stool or counter so that he must aim for the stool as a landing ledge in order to get at the reward. Allow your arm to slide up and down so that the reward is an enticement for him to jump onto the stool or counter. When he finally makes the jump, give him the reward instantly and praise him. It is important that you offer the food reward immediately after he performs properly so that he associates the command with the reward. It is equally important that you praise him instantly after the food reward is given, for the same reason. Repeat this sequence of *stimulus-response-reward-praise* five times and then quit. Conduct another session one or two hours later and repeat the procedure. Do this for several days until the kitten is performing the command on cue.

Step 5. The last phase of this series is getting the kitten to respond to the sequence of commands: *come when called, sit, jump onto the stool, sit and jump down.* Repeat the previous four steps. When the kitten gets up onto the stool or counter and is given his reward for doing so, give him the command "Sit." He should respond readily. When he does, give him a food reward immediately and praise him. Let him remain seated on the stool for about fifteen seconds. Hold out a food reward in your hand, down near the floor (sliding your arm back and forth as before). Say his name and "Down." When he jumps down (it will be for the reward), kneel and instantly give him the food treat and praise him lavishly and lovingly. Repeat this five times, then quit. Repeat the procedure an hour later. Repeat this lesson every day until the cat performs it every time on cue. It should not take too long.

Silly tricks only tend to demean a dignified cat; you may consider your kitten trained if he can do what has been offered within this chapter. Congratulations.

TEN

THE SHORT AND SWEET
PROBLEM SOLVER

This is a kitten fixer-upper for the perplexed pet owner. When a first-time cat owner howls, "I just got a kitten. What do I do?" and bangs the wall in frustration and bewilderment, it isn't a joke, although at times it's hard to keep from laughing. Kitten problems are only funny to those who don't have them. Here is a primer for the puzzled.

Some of the most common behavior problems people experience with kittens include peeing on the bed, dashing through the house in the middle of the night; digging scratches into your precious DVDs, and chewing on your house plants. Worse yet, your kitten may be going potty in your flower pots, eating and vomiting, not eating and vomiting, and hiding from you. These are but a few of your early kitten problems, and believe it or not, they are not terribly serious. Here are some uncomplicated solutions for uncomplicated problems.

Stop That Cat!

When your kitten misbehaves, especially in a destructive way, you must be able to stop him instantly and carry him away from the scene of the crime. This pertains to shredding the curtains, eating a house plant, getting into poisonous household cleaning products, and you name the rest. In your arsenal of Stop That Cat methods, the simplest is the most obvious. It is the use of the word *no*. Well, not so fast. It isn't *that* simple. By the strictest definition, *no*, is not really a command. It is more of a demand. It is also an important discipline tool. When you say, "No," your kitten should stop what he is doing instantly in response to the demand in your voice.

No, is, of course, the most negative-sounding word in the English language. It is very useful when applied properly. It can also screw up your relationship with a kitten if not applied with good sense. The object of using this one-word demand is to stop unwanted behavior before it becomes a behavior pattern. You must do this with a firm but loving authority and uncompromising consistency. You must catch a kitten in the act if you are going to reprimand him in a way that creates an aversion to the unwanted behavior. You may need to use a sharp-sounding voice or a loud noise or both. Most kittens are startled by loud, sudden noises and will do whatever is necessary to stop them, even if it means stopping what they are doing. A loud or sharp "No" will get his attention and signal your displeasure. It's a good start.

When your kitten misbehaves and you catch him in the act, you may do one of three things. All three actions disturb your kitten's senses: 1) say "No" in a firm tone of voice; 2) squirt a gentle stream of water at him (not in the face) with a plant sprayer or water pistol; or 3) slap your hand loudly with a magazine or newspaper (or even get his attention by stamping your foot on the floor). You may need to use a combination of these methods because some kittens do not get the message easily.

Despite the intensity of these actions, it is important that your kitten not interpret any of them as an expression of anger or, God forbid, a threat of violence. There is an important distinction between frightening your kitten and getting his attention by surprising him. Frightening your kitten will get you nothing and can in the long run make him distant with you as he grows into an adult cat. It is also mean-spirited.

After you have used one of these three methods, the next step is to scoop him up in your arms and grasp him by the nape of his neck the way a mama cat would, hold him tightly in midair with his hind legs supported by your open palm, and gently shake him. As you do this say, "No. No. No." Do not shake the kitten's head. Do this with loving authority so that there can be no mistake about your determination or your affection. This action establishes you as the top cat in the family; because it replicates the manner in which the mother cat chastises her kittens, it is perfectly acceptable as well as effective.

Administer the demand "No" in this fashion for all unacceptable behavior and for healthy cats of all ages. But wait. There's more.

Because your objective is to create within the kitten an acceptable behavior pattern, it is now time to teach him what to do to replace the unwanted behavior. In the case of scratching furniture, for example, after the "No. No. No," carry the furry offender to his scratch post. Stand him up in front of it and gently squeeze his front paws until his nails show. Rub them into the material of the post, teaching him where he may scratch without provoking you. Bear in mind that a cat scratches as a natural way to sharpen his nails and remove dead tissue. This behavior is necessary; the only question is where he may or may not do it. A kitten may also be attempting to mark his territory when he scratches the wall, the furniture, or even your curtains. You must *redirect* this activity to an acceptable location. Once you've redirected the kitten's activity, give him lavish vocal praise for doing the correct thing (even if you did it for him). You may even use a food reward. Try rubbing the scratch post with catnip for a little added reinforcement to the demand.

Another unwanted behavior is attacking and destroying house plants. Because some plants are toxic to cats, the kitten can harm himself as well as the plant, although it is quite natural for a cat to nibble on greenery. When people allow their cats to roam freely outdoors, the cats can chomp on grass and have no difficulty other than vomiting it up. Inside your home, you must give the demand "No. No. No." when you catch the kitten in the act of chewing on your favorite plant or using it for a toilet. Repeat the techniques outlined

above. The best way to redirect a kitten's desire to eat plants is to supply him with his own plant that is acceptable for munching. There are commercial plant products, available specifically for cats, that grow in their own containers and are ideal. Among them is wheatgrass. These are available in pet supply outlets.

As a deterrent you may sprinkle cayenne pepper on your own plants (leaves, stems, and soil) and allow the reprimand to be a naturally created aversion. An effective alternative is to place a grid of adhesive strips with a sticky texture that easily and humanely repels cats and kittens. Commercially manufactured and sold as Sticky Paws for Plants, it is recommended by the ASPCA as well as by *Consumer Reports* magazine as a humane product that really deters cats from misbehaving and makes it unnecessary to declaw them. For more information, see www.stickypaws.com. This product is also made for furniture and other areas a kitten likes to abuse.

Another option is to use your plant spray on the kitten to stop unwanted behavior, as you say "No." Then pick him up as described before and say "No. No. No." as you gently shake him. Take him to his own plant or give him a cat toy. Redirection is absolutely essential and a verbal or food reward plus praise should immediately follow. Remember, you want to discourage some patterns of behavior as you create others.

There are other techniques for dealing with unwanted behaviors. If your kitten has a tendency to chew or scratch clothing, lamp cords or anything else, simply coat the valued object with a commercially manufactured bitter-tasting product or with commercial hot sauce such as Tabasco. The unpleasant taste experience may stop the chewing problem. If a cat has chosen to use the arm of a sofa to shed his old nails, tape four or five tightly inflated balloons to the spot. The movement of the balloons may be enough to stop the average kitten. If not, when the first balloon pops from being mauled with the kitten's nails, the sound should be startling enough to send kitty hopping away. Be sure to remove the broken balloon.

To Pee or Not to Pee

What does it mean if your kitten suddenly stops using the litter pan? What if your kitten is urinating or defecating on the floor, the carpet, the sofa, or even your bed? What's that all about? Of all the problems cat owners face at one time or another, soiling your house is probably the most upsetting and perplexing, and for many it's hard to understand.

Assuming your kitten has been using the litter pan properly and then suddenly starts toileting on the floor, you must control your feelings and not react with anger or despair. Most people are offended by the sight of pee or poop outside the litter pan and feel betrayed by their beloved friend. The first thing to do is clean it up. The second is to try and figure out why it happened so that you can find the correct solution for the problem.

It could be a medical problem. A kitten that is not using his litter pan and is lethargic or not eating may be sick and should see a veterinarian, if only to rule out a medical problem. Among the various medical conditions that can cause this misbehavior are bladder infections, urinary blockages, kidney problems, and diabetes.

Maybe it's a territory thing. When a cat sprays or marks its territory (your home) with urine, it is making a claim of ownership for all other cats to know about. This behavior can be intertwined with sexual spraying on vertical objects, usually a wall. Unaltered (not castrated) male cats by five or six months of age will sooner or later back up against a vertical surface such as a door or furniture leg and spray a stream of scented urine against it. This is the beginning of sexual maturity.

Females and even some castrated males will also use scented urine for this purpose, but they are likely to do it in a squatting position. The most logical and the most desirable solution available is surgical neutering (castration) of male cats and *spaying* (ovariohysterectomy) of female cats. Having males or females sexually altered is likely to solve the problem, although it may persist if a pattern of behavior has already been established. Even so, surgery will certainly reduce its intensity. The best way to avoid this problem altogether is to have kittens sexually altered at an early age, before this behavior begins. Ask your veterinarian about when to have the procedure performed. Many vets believe it is fine to operate at two months of age while others feel it is better to wait until the cat is six months of age.

It could be due to anxiety or emotional stress. Cats and kittens that are frightened, plagued with nervousness, or upset about something specific will suddenly and without warning pee and poop on the floor, in the bathtub, on your bed, or on the sofa. It is an expression of their emotional state. Many things can upset a family cat, but a major cause is change in the family routine or composition.

House soiling often begins soon after you've brought a second cat into the house. It should come to an end within a few days as the two cats adjust to each other. It may be best to give the newcomer a separate litter pan in another room to respect the senior cat's territory. The same goes for food bowls. Always give the original resident first consideration for attention and territory. Place one or both cats in separate cat cages or in separate rooms. Allow the cage door or door to the other room to be open. Allow the new pet to walk

freely into the situation. There may be some hissing and spitting along with raised hackles, but this will soon end. The
cats will gradually investigate each other and eventually
come to a peaceable adjustment.

If a move to a new home is causing the problem, try to
understand that there is no greater cause of anxiety for a cat
than moving into a new house. It is all connected to the importance a cat places on his territory. It is almost impossible
to prevent this from happening. Have the litter pan placed at
a location convenient for you *but never near the front door or
window*, to prevent running away. Teach your cat to use the
litter pan all over again, as if he had never been trained before. Exercise patience and understanding in all matters, but
under no circumstances should you allow the cat out of the
house. There is always a strong possibility that he will run off
to find his old home and you may never see him again.

A change in the family structure can upset a cat just as it
might a child. When married couples separate or divorce and
one or the other person is gone, a cat may become upset and
start house soiling as an emotional expression. Problems can
arise when any member of the family leaves home, such as
when a child goes off to college or sleepaway camp. Certainly, the worst situation is when there is a death in the family. Like other members of the family, the cat will need
consolation and extra attention and affection.

What to Do When Your Cat Stops Using the Litter Pan

1. Keep the litter pan clean. A cat or kitten will not use it
   if urine and solid waste are not cleaned out frequently.
   Scoop the solids out at least twice a day and replace
   the litter material entirely once or twice a week. When
   you do this, wash the pan with soap and water.
2. Try changing the brand or the type of litter in the pan.

There is an incredible variety of choices available, and your cat just may prefer one type to another.

3. Once your kitten has used another area for his toilet outside the pan, it is essential to eliminate his odor from these locations thoroughly. Use a high-quality odor neutralizer meant for this purpose, not detergent, perfume, soap and water, and definitely not household ammonia, which contains an ingredient that is present in urine and will actually attract the cat. By obliterating the scent of the urine or feces, you will help prevent the cat from returning to the scene of the crime and repeating it. There are many odor neutralizers sold for this purpose in pet supply outlets.

4. Give your cat added affection, play, exercise, and food treats.

5. If you catch your kitten in the act of eliminating outside the litter pan, use the plant spray or water gun and squirt him (not in the face), say "No" in a firm tone of voice, as described above, and carry him off to his litter pan. Give him a food reward after he uses the pan properly.

6. To avoid use of the bathtub as a toilet, fill it with about two inches of water until the problem stops. Few kittens enjoy standing in water.

7. Confine the cat to one room until the problem comes to an end.

8. In a multicat household, be sure to have more than one litter pan.

9. Have your cat surgically altered. (Males are neutered and females are spayed.)

10. Use common sense and ingenuity. To prevent your kitten from returning to the same spot he has been soiling, cover it with a large piece of furniture so he cannot re-mark it, which is what cats (and dogs) feel

compelled to do. If you see him going near the same location, scoop him up in your arms and take him to his litter pan. Give him a food reward and verbal praise. If your cat backs up against a wall or other vertical object, again, take him to his litter pan. If he behaves this way at the front or back door, it usually means he detects the scent of another cat, which will compel him to scent-mark his territory with urine. Find a way to discourage strange cats from coming to your door. Use a manufactured cat repellent for this purpose, or seal off the cracks in the door to prevent the odor from seeping through.

11. Sometimes you can solve a litter-pan problem by simply reminding your kitten where the pan is and reinstructing him how to use it. Repeat the procedure many times and use a food reward and verbal praise each time you do.

Scratching

What appears to be spiteful, mischievous, destructive behavior in cats is nothing more than an innocent need created by their unique nails. When a cat scratches your furniture, carpeting, or curtains, he is obeying an important instinct to remove the outer sheath or covering of his nails. The cat must remove this outer layer of tissue as new nail tissue continues to grow underneath. This destructive behavior diminishes when you trim your kitten's nails for him and provide an acceptable scratching surface. It is also advisable to apply one of various techniques available for discouraging this behavior.

It is essential to trim your kitten's nails frequently for several reasons. First, it helps to remove the outer nail sheath and allow the incoming nails to emerge without discomfort.

Second, it minimizes destructive behavior toward your furniture and various possessions because you will have removed the need to scratch. Third, once the kitten's claws are trimmed, humans are less likely to be scratched.

A kitten's claws are unique because they are retractable and do not show in their usual, retracted position. When cats walk, only the tips come in contact with the ground. The claws are, however, formidable weapons that extend when the cat prepares to fight, run, or climb. They are also unsheathed when the cat is frightened or panicked. Unsheathed claws are also necessary for catching prey animals; they are what make cats the consummate hunters of the animal kingdom. Tree climbing, jumping, escape maneuvers, playing, fighting, mating, and many other activities and behaviors all involve the retractable claws we tactfully call nails.

In addition, a cat claims territory and makes his presence known by marking with visible scratches the ground or various vertical objects (as well as by leaving behind his urine scent). This is deeply embedded instinctive behavior and is impossible to eradicate. The best you can do is redirect his scratching to an acceptable area and create an aversion to scratching objects that are not acceptable. Refer to the section "Stop That Cat!" at the beginning of the chapter for instructions on how to redirect scratching behavior. Bear in mind that after stopping your kitten from scratching the wrong things, you must take him to where it is acceptable to scratch, such as a scratch post or disposable scratch pad.

There are some cat owners who believe that having a cat declawed is the answer to feline scratching problems. However, a large majority of cat lovers and serious cat people have the humane attitude that declawing is disabling and disfiguring. They argue that a cat's claws are indispensable. Most serious cat breeders, exhibitors, and cat registering organizations discourage people from applying this medical procedure to any cat.

There is a misconception that declawing is the surgical removal of a cat's nails. In reality, it is an amputation of the digits, comparable to removing fingers, not just the nails. National registry organizations such as the Cat Fanciers' Association (CFA) do not allow declawed cats to compete in cat shows sanctioned by them primarily because they believe that such cats have been purposely deformed. There are a number of alternatives for addressing the issue of destructive scratching without resorting to this drastic measure, the most effective being to trim your cat's nails on a frequent basis.

No matter which solution you choose to diminish your kitten's scratching behavior, the most important thing you can do is learn how to trim your kitten's nails. Nothing helps solve this problem more than blunting the nails and removing the need for the cat to scratch away the outer sheath. See Chapter Seven, "Grooming Your Kitten."

Every kitten needs something designed especially for him to scratch. Get him a scratch post, a disposable scratch pad, or a piece of carpeted cat furniture, as described in Chapter Four, "What to Buy for Your Kitten."

Teaching your kitten to use a scratch post or scratch pad. Apply these techniques every day and as often as you can stand it. When you find your kitten scratching anyplace other than the post or the pad, you must stop him by saying, "No," or squirting him with a plant spray or water pistol (not in the face). Then pick him up and hold him by the nape of the neck (as his mother would). Hold him out in midair with the bottom feet supported by the flat of your other hand, and gently shake him. Say, "No. No. No," in a firm yet soft tone of voice. Immediately take him to the scratch post or the disposable scratch pad or to his carpeted cat furniture. Set him down, place his front paws on the scratching surface, and move them up and down as if teaching him to scratch. Having done this, give him a food treat and lovingly praise him.

Eventually, saying "No" in a firm tone of voice will suffice without all the rest. Once you begin discipline with "No," always use that word exclusively for that purpose and no other. In this way, the word becomes an effective training tool. Always say "No" with a resonant tone of voice so your cat will always recognize its meaning.

Create an aversion to your furniture. The idea is to get your kitten to avoid your furniture as a place to stretch and scratch. One way is to simply cover the areas of the furniture that your kitten enjoys scratching with thick sheets of plastic so that they are unpleasant and dissatisfying for scratching purposes. You can also affix lots of balloons to the area so that one or more balloons will make a loud popping noise when scratched and startle the kitten. This noise should create an aversion to the furniture.

Another technique is to use a commercial product manufactured with an adhesive on both sides, which is available in strips, in sheets, and on a pull-out roll. Called Sticky Paws, it goes a long way to solving this problem. Cats hate the feel of the adhesive on their paws and so tend to leave it alone. The ASPCA and *Consumer Reports* magazine both endorse this superior product because of its effectiveness and kindness to the cat.

When Cats Bite

It's hard to look down at your sweet little kitty cat and think of him as a potential source of pain, and yet some kittens (and adult cats) have the potential to hurt you or another cat. A cat bite is not the same as a dog bite. A wound from a cat punctures the skin and goes deep into the tissue for the entire length of the teeth. A dog bite is usually more of a slash and tear, although it can involve shallow punctures as well. The puncture wound of a cat is painful and takes longer to heal because the tissue damaged is too deep to be stitched up. Also, the potential for having bacteria injected into your system is great. When a cat bites another cat, there is usually an abscess or large swelling from an infection that develops at the bite area. Even a kitten's bite, although rarely severe, can hurt because their teeth are like sharp needles. When a kitten bites, he often scratches you as well for good measure.

Most aggression in domestic cats, however, is directed toward other domestic cats or toward their prey animals. It is morbidly fascinating that when cats stalk and capture a prey animal, there does not seem to be the anger and the fury involved that we see when cats attack or challenge each other or defend themselves. Dispatching a captured mouse or bird is a dispassionate act born from an instinct to hunt for food. It is almost peaceful—but not quite, if you happen to be the mouse. One cannot deny, however, that a cat stalking is a dramatic and riveting sight.

Aggressive behavior not directed toward prey can be the sign of a medical problem or of emotional stress. Aggressive behavior may stem from environmental situations such as human abuse or abuse from a dog, from other cats in a household, or from other kittens in a litter. The end result of abuse can be shyness or aggression, both of which stem from feelings of fear.

Cat-to-Human Aggression

Defensive aggression. If your kitten or adult cat feels threatened by you or believes he is in danger, he will instinctively scratch or bite you, or both. This can happen if you try to place him in a travel carrier when he doesn't want to go in it, for example, or if you attempt to hold him in a way that upsets him. When you corner a cat, he will take a defensive posture and lash out with his nails and teeth. Most cat bites are defensive in nature, although not always justified or appropriate. Once the threat is over, his hostile behavior subsides. This same behavior is also seen with other cats and dogs that are threatening.

Pain aggression. Pain can be an important source of aggression, but the aggression only lasts as long as the pain lasts. If you hit a cat, pull at him, or hold him in a manner that hurts him, he will instinctively scratch or bite. If you pull a cat's tail during play or grab his fur, he will respond in an aggressive manner, but it is usually an instantaneous outburst that comes to a quick end.

Play aggression. Hiding and suddenly pouncing, stalking, or attacking human ankles are all part of play behavior despite the fact that a kitten can get rough and use its nails and needle-sharp teeth on you. These are behaviors most commonly indulged in by kittens as a form of acting out and practicing for future adult situations, which in domesticity never really happen. Despite the fact that these actions may

be painless and amusing, they should be corrected and redirected to appropriate toys. Imagine these same behaviors when your kitten becomes an adult and can really hurt you.

Love bites. Some cats and kittens will gently bite your finger as you stroke or pet them in a loving manner. Adult cats may hold a part of your hand firmly but gently between their teeth as you pet them, but they do not break the skin. It seems to be similar to the nape bite that is used by males to hold females in position during copulation: this too is an inhibited bite that does not break the skin. Love bites are one of those feline mysteries for which we will never get a definitive explanation.

Aggression triggered by illness. Humans may find themselves scratched or severely bitten by a cat when the animal is suffering from one of various medical conditions such as brain tumors, constricted blood flow within the brain, rabies, or toxoplasmosis (a parasitic disease).

WHAT TO DO ABOUT AGGRESSIVE BEHAVIOR

It is important to stop a kitten from being aggressive and scratching and biting no matter how painless and cute it may seem. When kittens scratch, nip, or bite, they must be corrected as described in the section "Stop That Cat!" earlier in this chapter. It is important to stop these unacceptable behaviors early so that they do not become habits.

Separate your cats. In a multicat household, it may be necessary to keep fighting cats apart from each other in separate rooms or in two cat cages or travel carriers until they make an adjustment. For the best results place the cages or carriers at opposite ends of the same room where the cats can see each other. Each day move the cats closer together. This will give them an opportunity to gradually adjust to each other's presence without doing harm. Let the cats out of the cages at feeding time only. Place the bowls just outside each cage. Close all doors so that you can return them to the cages once they have eaten and used their litter pans. This should establish the association of meals as a reward for accepting each other's presence. When the cages or carriers can be side by side without any signs of aggression, the cats are ready to have the run of the house.

Changing behavior with the help of prescribed drugs. When all else fails and you cannot control your cat's aggressive behavior, you have the last-resort option of talking to a veterinarian about it. Most vets are able to prescribe drug therapy for fear-related aggression, territorial and sexual aggression, compulsive eating behaviors, and even for urine marking. A qualified doctor of veterinary medicine who can evaluate an individual cat based on the animals' problem, his age, environment, weight, and general condition must be the one to determine the proper drug and its dosage. Bear in mind that there may be side effects and contraindications with each drug depending on an individual cat's response to it. This is why a trained professional must monitor a cat on drug therapy. The use of such therapy for behavioral problems is an ever-changing and somewhat controversial approach. Most professionals will agree that pharmacologic intervention in feline behavior problems should be considered as an adjunct to behavior modification and not a solution in and of itself. Behavior modification as offered in the preceding pages must be considered as the primary approach to problem solving.

Eating Problems

Refusing to eat. When it comes to being finicky about food, cats get bad press. There are overblown TV commercials showing cats turning up their noses at some unappetizing gruel while running to gourmet-type foods being served in crystal dessert goblets. The truth is that refusing to eat may have nothing at all to do with the menu but may be a medical problem or an emotional problem caused by a stressful situation. In addition, some cats cannot or will not eat when they are in a new or strange environment, such as a boarding situation, overnight at the vet's clinic, or when accompanying the family on an out-of-town visit. Refusal to eat is most often caused by fear, depression, anxiety, or worry over some change in the cat's routine.

Failing to eat for more than a few days could also be a sign of a medical problem, which should be diagnosed by a veterinarian. Disorders of the lips, wounds, medical problems within the mouth, internal infection, abscess, fever, metabolic disorders, intestinal obstruction, injury, and tumors are all potential causes for a lack of appetite or unwillingness to eat. A veterinarian may approach the problem with appetite stimulants, tranquilizers, vitamin therapy, or, in extreme medical situations, with forced feeding techniques.

Nevertheless, most often kittens or cats that refuse to eat simply do not like what they are being fed. They may prefer dry food to moist or moist to dry. They may not like the brand, the contents, the texture, or they may simply be getting you to jump through hoops. Never underestimate the cleverness of a cat. If you feed him table scraps or doctor his regular ration, you may inadvertently create a pattern that may be impossible to break. When a kitten or adult cat goes on a hunger strike, he can hold out long after you finally give in to whatever it is that he wants. You may find yourself becoming the personal chef for a cat for years.

To avoid creating a finicky eater, feed your cat a variety of tastes and flavors of premium commercial cat food. There are a number of different flavored types available to maintain the interest of just about any kitten or cat. Dry foods are the most convenient, the most economical, and, with some brands, the most tasty from the cat's point of view. You can alternate between dry and canned food or mix the two together. What you feed your kitten from the beginning will set the tone for the rest of his life.

Overeating. Obesity can be a serious problem. Obesity in cats has the same negative effects for health and well-being as it does in humans. Fat cats are more prone to heart disease, respiratory conditions, kidney failure, osteoarthritis, digestive failure, diabetes, and infections. Obesity also makes surgery more difficult for cats.

Obesity is caused by endocrine disorders, inability to metabolize large quantities of food (usually in aging cats), and simple overfeeding. There are circumstances in a cat's life when a greater quantity of food is required, such as when the cat is pregnant, nursing kittens, growing rapidly in kittenhood, or living in colder regions.

Avoiding obesity is almost always achieved by obtaining a veterinarian's feeding instructions and sticking to them. *Feed your kitten a normal diet and nothing more.* Feed your cat according to a consistent schedule, the same times every day. Offer few between-meals snacks, using treats in moderation for rewards when training or problem solving.

In the Middle of the Night

Whenever a new kitten owner discusses the furry blessed event of the family, the subject of strange nocturnal behavior comes up. It has been dubbed "the Midnight Special" by some and "the cat crazies" by others. It usually goes like this: Late at night, after the family has gone to bed and are in a sound sleep, they are awakened by a sudden crash. It could be a lamp falling over or the trash can tipping to the side. Out of a cloud of dust comes the thundering sound of pouncing paws as the feline night stalker races across the entire house, up one wall and down again. The kitten stops at the highest point he can climb and lets out a chest-beating *mmrrrowl* at the top of his voice, roaring like a tiny lion, and then begins to run again. Only this time he runs sideways, stops in the middle of the room, leaps straight off the ground, and pounces down with all his might. This can go on for fifteen truly disturbing minutes. When the dust settles, the family can go back to sleep . . . unless the kitten starts it all over again.

Kittens, young cats, and even some older ones are remarkably playful, especially at night. There is surely a perfectly logical reason for this, but we have yet to figure out exactly what it is! The behavior often begins with a full use of the litter pan and may be a statement of pride about what the kitten has just accomplished in the litter pan. There are some good guesses about why this behavior happens in the middle of the night. It seems to be connected to the reaffirmation of territory. From a practical standpoint, the kitten has the unobstructed run of the house once the family has gone to bed. Darkness is also in the mix, since cats have the unique ability to concentrate dim light and see quite well in shadowy rooms. They sleep much of the day and may have what can only be described as an overflow of energy at night. In addition, a kitten can really cut loose without being observed or stopped by giants with far-reaching arms and hands.

Some of this nocturnal activity is the drama of play ritual, which is a rehearsal for hunting methods, fighting behavior, escape behavior, and sexual activity as well as simply fun for its own sake. The feline technique for hunting is to stalk and ambush and then pounce, utilizing maximum energy in an instantaneous rush of bursting effort. All of these behaviors can be seen in the midnight crazies. Kittens habitually use even more energy in play than they would when actually hunting. It is little wonder that their nocturnal behavior tends to keep their families awake. Worse yet, the play can become destructive to various possessions, such as the lamps and knickknacks that crash to the ground.

Excessive nighttime play occurs when the family does not actively initiate play behavior during the day or when the kitten is continually confined in small quarters without much human attention. To undercut this late show, provide your kitten with more opportunities for a variety of play activities. Toss around a crumpled piece of paper as if it were a ball.

Relax. Once kittenhood is over, you no longer need to shout, "What do I do?" It's now time to prepare for the ease and comfort of life with an adult cat. Yeah, right.

That'll get his engine going. Ping Pong balls are among the feline's favorite toys. But play needn't always be interactive between kitten and human. It can also involve toys that cats can play with themselves, such as a wooden thread spool, a ball, or a squeak toy, imbued with catnip. Of course, a companion pet is a good answer providing they get along.

When kittens live together, they find an infinite number of games to play with each other. At times, they have mock fights and appear to wrestle with one another. At other times, they will share a toy and take turns batting it around. Some pairs of kittens will run together or try to annoy one another. As they mature, they develop a hierarchy and one emerges as the top cat, getting its way over the other. However, this sometimes changes. Kittens are delightful together but are also double trouble. Some people love the kitten experience so much that they quickly bring in another. If you're up for it, you will laugh twice as much, you will love twice as much. You will also clean up twice as much.

Having read these pages carefully and completely you should now know what to do with your new kitten. You have answered the question in the title. Nevertheless, your new friend will remain a kitten for at least the first year, and perhaps for the rest of his life. Keep the book handy and use it as you would any other owner's manual. If you're smart, and you probably are, do not let your kitten get his paws on it or sink his teeth into it.

Suggested Reading

Behavior

Beadle, Muriel. *The Cat: A Complete Authoritative Compendium of Information About Domestic Cats.* New York: Simon & Schuster, 1977.

Christensen, Wendy. *Outwitting Cats: Tips, Tricks, and Techniques for Persuading the Felines in Your Life That What You Want Is Also What They Want.* Guilford, Conn.: The Lyons Press, 2004.

Leyhausen, Paul. *Cat Behavior: The Predatory and Social Behavior of Domestic and Wild Cats.* New York and London: Garland STPM Press, 1979.

Smythe, R. H., M.R.C.V.S. *Cat Psychology.* Neptune, N.J.: T.F.H. Publication, 1978.

Cat Care

Shojai, Amy D. *Complete Kitten Care.* New York: New American Library, 2002.

Siegal, Mordecai, and CFA and Its Associates. *The Cat Fanciers' Association Complete Cat Book: The Official Publication of the CFA.* New York: HarperCollins, 2004.

Siegal, Mordecai. *Simon & Schuster's Guide to Cats.* New York: Simon & Schuster, 1983.

Medical

Carlson, Delbert G., DVM, and James Giffin, MD. *Cat Owner's Home Veterinary Handbook*. New York: Howell Book House, 1995.

Eldredge, Debra, DVM. *Pills for Pets*. New York: Citadel Press, 2003.

Shojai, Amy D. *Pet Care in the New Century*. New York: New American Library, 2001.

Siegal, Mordecai, and the Faculty, Staff, and Associates, Cornell Feline Health Center, Cornell University. *The Cornell Book of Cats*. Second edition. New York: Villard, 1997.

Training

Johnson-Bennett, Pam. *Think Like a Cat. How to Raise a Well-Adjusted Cat, Not a Sour Puss*. New York: Penguin Books, 2002.

Rhea, Alice. *Good Cats, Bad Habits: The Complete A-to-Z Guide for When Your Cat Misbehaves*. New York: Fireside, 1995.

Miscellaneous Subjects

Balliner, Maryjean. *Cat Massage: A Whiskers-to-Tail Guide to Your Cat's Ultimate Petting Experience*. New York: St. Martin's, 1997.

Shojai, Amy D. *Your Aging Cat*. New York: New American Library, 2003.

Wright, Michael, and Sally Walters. *The Book of the Cat*. New York: Summit Books, 1980.

Index